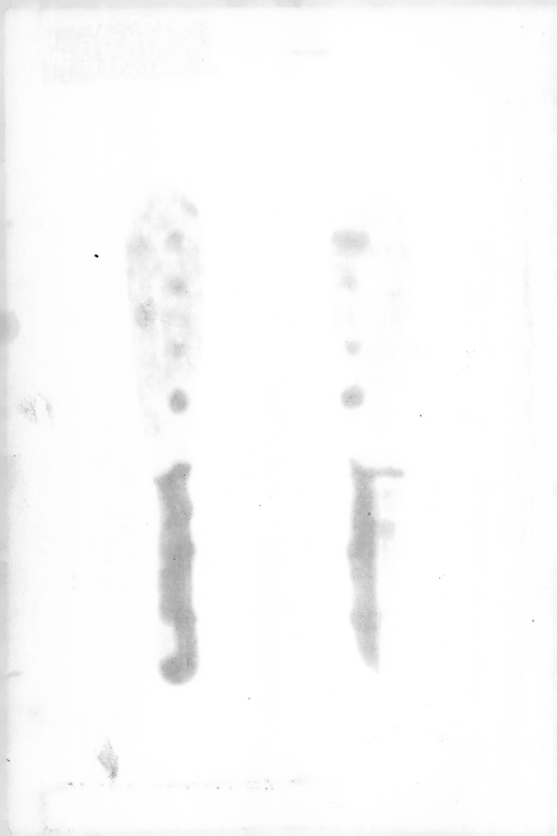

Books by Kurt Unkelbach

ADULT
Love on a Leash
The Winning of Westminster
Murphy
The Pleasures of Dog Ownership *(with his wife)*
The Love That Shook the World

JUVENILE
The Dog in My Life
Ruffian: International Champion
Both Ends of the Leash
A Cat and His Dogs
The Dog Who Never Knew
Catnip: Selecting and Training Your Cat
You're a Good Dog, Joe
How to Bring Up Your Pet Dog

HOW TO BRING

KURT UNKELBACH
Illustrated by Sam Savitt

UP YOUR
PET DOG

**Choosing
Understanding
Training
Protecting
Enjoying**

DODD, MEAD & COMPANY · NEW YORK

ACKNOWLEDGMENTS

For assistance in making this book as valid and as up-to-date as possible, the author wishes to thank Aennchen Antonelli, Henry Bernacki, Julie Brown, John Brownell, Lloyd Case, Raymond Church, VMD, James Corbin, Janet Mack, John Mara, DVM, Evelyn Monte, Seymour Prager, Maxwell Riddle, and Armour Wood, VMD.

Also, the American Kennel Club, American Veterinary Medical Association, Cornell Research Laboratory for Diseases of the Dog, Dog Fanciers Club, Kennel Club (England), National Research Council, and the several dog food companies named herein.

And special thanks to my wife, Evie, our daughter, Cary, and our many dogs, past and present.

To Wentzle Ruml, Jr.

Contents

Follow most of the advice in this book and your dog will become the best friend you've ever had. It answers the many letters from my readers.

A Foreword That Is Not to Be Skipped

WHEN I STARTED writing books about dogs, I had no way of knowing that much of my future writing time would be devoted to answering letters from readers who had purchased, borrowed or somehow managed to read my books.

The majority of the letter writers seem to be under voting age, and I assume this is because voters feel that time will remedy anything, including the faults of their dogs. That is wishful thinking. While every puppy is born with great pet potential, the owner must take a hand in shaping that potential. Otherwise, the end result is a tail-wagging nuisance and not a joy.

There's nothing difficult about raising and training a dog. Like man, *canis familiaris* is a social animal and a firm believer in family life. If a dog can't live with other dogs, he's just as happy living with people. The reverse, of course, is also true, and many a lonely person owns several dogs.

The pages of this book will tell you everything you really need to know about your dog. Follow some of the advice and you'll have a more obedient, healthier pet. Follow most of it and your dog will become the best friend you've ever had. Follow all of it and you'll save money, and—if you're ambitious—discover a few ways to make money.

I must confess that much of the advice found herein is not traditional and will not be found elsewhere. But it is all based on experience and the repeated inquiries of my friends and read-

1

ers. It has worked for me, and it will work for you.

The pages also break with tradition in another way: the names of the pure breeds are capitalized. The American Kennel Club considers the pure breeds to be proper breeds and thus entitled to proper, capitalized names. Webster does not. If your Uncle Louie is a grammarian with purist tendencies, he may object. In such a case, please don't give him my address. Tell Uncle Louis to send any complaints to the american kennel club.

1

Your Dog

FIRST THINGS first, and the first thing to understand about your dog is that he is nowhere nearly as intelligent as you are. If you have been able to read this far, and never mind how poor your school grades are, that's more than he can do.

This does not mean that your dog is an inferior being. As domestic animals go, he's the brightest of the lot: smarter than the horse, much smarter than the cat, and a genius compared to cattle, goats, sheep and hogs.

As with humans, some dogs do fall below the norm. These dullards still make fine pets. It just requires a little more time and patience to train them. But even a dullard's natural instincts are superior to yours, and so are most of his senses.

Pound for pound, he's stronger and faster than you, and his reflexes make you seem muscle-bound. All good reasons why an ambitious child should not try to train an Irish Wolfhound, the 130-pounder who is the tallest of the breeds (thirty-three inches at the withers).

A dog's vision is about on a par with yours, in that he can see just as far down the road. While he can't define a distant object as well, he can see more without turning his head, since the set of his eyes gives him a wider field of vision. And your dog's eyes have another big advantage: third lids that slide over the eyes in times of danger. A debatable disadvantage is his color blindness,

A young child should not try to train an Irish Wolfhound.

and this depends on how you feel about color television: a dog
sees everything in various shades of white, gray and black. When
a dog favors a red pillow over a blue one, his preference is based
on feel and smell. Red and blue are blobs of black to him.

Your taste buds are superior to a dog's, but not your senses of
hearing and smelling. For a dog, the world is a very noisy, scent-
ridden place. So, in a way, it's a miracle that he fits so well into
the average household. He's an exceptionally tolerant animal.

All of the above applies to your dog, whether he's a purebred
or a mixed breed. The important thing to remember is that his

4

brain power is much less than yours. So, from the very beginning of your association, you are the responsible party. You are the boss, and the sooner you establish that fact in your dog's mind, the happier you and your dog will be.

In the beginning of most human-canine relationships, dogs come to their new homes as puppies. Let's sample some pup questions that pop up in the minds of most dog lovers:

I have been promised a puppy for Christmas. Which sex do you recommend?

There are pros and cons for both sexes, so most canine authorities hedge on this question, but there's no question in my mind: a bitch (female) pup is always the best bet. Like a girl, a bitch

A dog sees everything in various shades of white, gray, and black.

develops faster (mentally and physically) than a male, so she adjusts earlier and responds earlier to training. And almost all of the time, her price tag is lower.

The only drawback is that a bitch usually comes in season (mating time) twice a year, and the first season can occur any time after she's six months old. The period lasts about three weeks, and all during it she's a bit messy around the house, and must be confined. (For more on the confinement of bitches in season, see INSIDE INFORMATION.) If you do want to breed her, it's always wisest to wait until her second season, when she is more fully developed.

If you don't intend to breed her, have her spayed. This is a simple operation for any veterinarian, and the end results are that the bitch will not be able to reproduce and will not come in season again. Despite published nonsense to the contrary, spaying (after the first season) does not adversely affect a bitch's future development, health, and longevity. Then there's the widely-held myth that a spayed bitch becomes fat and lazy. Whenever you see a fat dog of either sex, be sure he is overfed and not getting enough exercise. Nine times out of ten, his owner will be fat and lazy.

As for Christmas, that happens to be the worst time to bring a pup home. Every puppy is a baby, and he's sure to be confused by the noise, lights, excitement, and mobs of people around the home at holiday time. So wait until the annual bash is over and the household has returned to normal. The pup's seller will understand.

The ideal time for the pup's homecoming is when you have at least a week off from school—and the more weeks the better. If you're not around to care for him and establish your status as boss, his confusion will continue and he'll be more difficult to train.

Is there a correct puppy age for introducing him to his new home?

Yes, and it's from eight to ten weeks old. I've been around dogs for a long time, or for more years than some of the leading animal behaviorists have been on earth, and I agree with their research.

6

In a nutshell: like human babies, very young puppies do need mother love—until seven weeks of age, puppies rely mostly on natural instincts. They start thinking on their own at about eight weeks.

While his thinking doesn't amount to much then, it does enable a pup to start adjusting to new surroundings, to learn his name, and to understand that a rug is not a public bathroom.

Where does one go to find a quality pup?

Let's begin with the worst place to go in most cases: a pet shop. Almost always, the shop's puppies have been weaned too early and then shipped a great distance. In any event, the pups are treated as merchandise, often come from questionable breeders, and are usually overpriced. Pet shops depend on impulse sales: the pup looks forlorn, you want to make him happy, and time payments and all sorts of dubious guarantees are available. The exceptions are the fast-disappearing mom-and-pop pet shops, so-called because they are family-owned and have been in the same location for many years. Quite often, the owners are also breeders. Since they depend on a good local reputation, they can't afford to sell bum pups.

If you know the breed you want and have money in the bank, go to a reliable breeder. If you cannot locate such a breeder, write the American Kennel Club (AKC) for the names and addresses of the breeders in your area. (See SUPPLEMENTAL TIPS.)

No money in the bank? Visit the headquarters of your nearby humane societies and you'll find the right pup. One of the main objectives of these nonprofit societies is to find happy homes for their canine orphans.

But no matter where you look for your pup, it's wise to keep certain precautions in mind. (Check them out in INSIDE INFORMA-TION.)

I know that the American Kennel Club recognizes 116 pure breeds of dogs, but which breeds make the best pets?

That number 116 is a little misleading, since it really represents a grand total of individual breeds. All varieties of certain breeds are recognized as *one breed*. There is only one Boxer, for example, but there are three varieties of Poodles: Toy, Miniature, and Standard. All three varieties come under the one heading of Poodle. A given breed's varieties may be a matter of size, as with the Poodle, or a matter of coat, as with the Collie (Rough and Smooth).

For practical purposes, the A.K.C. has divided all 116 breeds, with their varieties, into six different groups. In five of these groups, several breeds make excellent pets and companions for young dog lovers. I am always willing to be brave at a distance, and you'll find my choices in SUPPLEMENTAL TIPS. Granted that they have been properly bred, pups of all these breeds will possess these virtues: high degree of canine intelligence, easy keepers (not finicky about food), even temperament, soundness, sufficient size for rough and tumble, simple coat care, and responsiveness— rather than stubbornness—to training. Who could ask for anything more?

As indicated at the start, in this book, intended for dog owners, we use the preferred spelling of the American Kennel Club, where every word of a breed name is capitalized. Take, for example, Bedlington Terrier or Irish Setter. According to Webster, it would be lower case for terrier and setter. That is for the scholarly!

Is there a right age for starting a puppy's training?

Yes, but that's a secret each pup keeps to himself. But if we are on the same wave length, then eight weeks, or whenever you bring the youngster home, is the time to start.

On the other hand, some of my friends who fancy the small breeds start puppy training as early as the fourth week, or as soon as the baby animal has been weaned. So a puppy can be started at any age, although there's never a guarantee that he'll catch on quickly. The training will have to proceed at his individual pace, and not in accordance with your own desires. Be sure of one thing: you can't rush a canine baby.

Now, I happen to breed Labrador Retrievers, so I usually keep a couple of pups from each litter. I can't recall two litter mates who progressed equally. Often, it has taken a single day to housebreak one pup, and four or five days to housebreak his litter mate.

Once a pup knows his name and is housebroken (matter of a week, at most), and then becomes accustomed to both collar and leash, he's ready to learn his basic commands. For best results, training should be by schedule (one command at a time), rather than by timetable. Always keep lessons short—a few minutes at the most—and full of fun for the pup. Praise even his shoddiest performance, and reward any brilliance with a tidbit. And never, never expect him to be perfect. He'll improve with age. Just as you will.

Forcing a pup to learn anything and severely disciplining him are old-fashioned training methods. Today, we know that the first seven months of a pup's life are critical, in that, during this time span, he develops the personality he will carry through the rest of his life. Shout at your pup or beat him, even non-severely, and you'll end up with a shy, nervous wreck—and maybe a fear biter. The big idea is to win his love and trust and keep him outgoing. So, when you're mad at the world or feeling out of sorts, skip the training session.

You'll find easy training methods up ahead.

Are any special preparations required before bringing a puppy home?

Not many, but a puppy is a little more trouble than a new canary in a cage.

Many pups are advertised as "housebroken," but any puppy will forget his manners in a new situation. So where to keep the pup until he is actually housebroken is the first problem.

In the average home, the most logical place is the kitchen. I confine my pups there by stringing a folding-type baby gate across the open doorway leading to the rest of the house. There are also puppy pens on the market, or you can make one yourself. (For the easy way, see INSIDE INFORMATION.) He stays in his pen when you are busy elsewhere. Shredded newspaper makes fine litter.

Fresh, clean drinking water should be available to him at all times. This means replenishing his supply at least five times a day, and room temperature is fine. The drinking pan doesn't have to be big, but it should be heavy, so that the pup can't tip it. Most pups like to plant their front feet in the water pan, and some like to play in the water, so expect plenty of splashing. Place a heavy thickness of newspaper under the pan to absorb the spilled water.

As the pup matures, his drinking habits become more orderly. But adult, whiskered dogs tend to dribble a bit, and there's no way of teaching a dog to use a napkin. One of my ten-year-old dogs has always been a slob indoors, so I keep a rubber mat under the water container. When he backs off from drinking, water

Most pups like to plant their front feet in the water pan.

whether she has ever been a mother or not, readily accepts a puppy of either sex. But no matter what the sex of the senior pet is, human affection should be distributed equally between the animals.

About half of the questions that arrive in my mailbox are related to puppy health. I think this is because many new and potential puppy owners are confused by the misinformation that is bandied about by self-appointed canine experts. The Aunt Tillie who remembers precisely about how she took care of her wonderful dog as a little girl has conveniently forgotten that her mother really took care of the dog, and that the dog lived only three years and not twelve. And Harry Glump "knows all about dogs" because his brother used to breed Bull Terriers. Or were they Bulldogs?

Thanks to veterinary research, the new knowledge about canine health has drastically changed beliefs that were firm only ten years ago. It would be difficult to convince the Aunt Tillies and Harry Glumps concerning the information you're going to read, but here are the important things to know about puppy health:

Distemper

This is one of several deadly canine diseases. There are many varieties of distemper, but all come under the same heading.

Granted that his dam is healthy, a puppy inherits from her about six weeks of immunity from distemper. Then, since a pup is not strong enough for the full, preventive vaccine, he is given a temporary shot. So don't bring home a pup who hasn't had his temporary shot.

Depend on your vet's advice for the permanent shots. I happen to favor the two-shot method. This calls for a shot between the ages of ten to twelve weeks, and a second shot four weeks later. These days, the permanent shots also protect against two other deadly canine diseases:

Hepatitis and Leptospirosis

Hepatitis destroys the liver, leptospirosis destroys the kidneys, and—like distemper—they are contagious. You are taking a very

13

big gamble if you neglect the permanent shots. They are usually combined with the distemper shots.

The word permanent is technical. It means that your dog is safe for a year, and maybe a little longer. To be on the sure side, visit your veterinarian annually for a booster shot. And forget about the pups who are advertised as having "lifetime shots." Not only misleading, but an utter falsehood.

Rabies

Some states require vaccination against rabies, so check the local laws. This is the "mad dog" disease and there's no cure in sight for it. If a rabid dog bites you, rush for the nearest doctor.

While rabies is not common, it's wise to inoculate your pup against it, especially if you live in the suburbs or the country. It is transmitted by the bite and saliva of animals already ill with rabies such as dogs, foxes, bats, rabbits, mice, rats, squirrels, skunks, raccoons, opossums, muskrats, and wildcats. A rabid animal goes mad, knows no fear, and bites anything in sight.

In my own case, I have my pups inoculated for rabies at about six months, and then every two years thereafter. But it's always wisest to follow your own vet's advice.

About half the pet dogs in America are never given any of the preventive shots recommended above. Of the remaining half, one half of them are never given booster shots. That is why the first three deadly diseases are still common, and why rabies is still a danger to dogs. Of course, the owners are at fault and not their dogs. Please do not join the ranks of the irresponsible.

Worms and Worming

No matter how healthy a pup looks, you can be almost certain that he is playing host to worms—if he has not been wormed. Even in the case of a fat and seemingly healthy puppy, you can be sure that he has worms.

Pups should be wormed after they are weaned, or at about five or six weeks. So don't buy a puppy who hasn't been wormed. Then, when you take the pup to the vet for his first permanent

14

shots, bring along one of his fresh stools in a jar. With the help of his microscope, the vet can determine whether your pup has worms or worm eggs.

Since a pup can be infested with one or more types of worms, it's nonsensical to save a little money by buying the worm medicines available at so many stores. Your pup's future health won't be helped if you treat him for roundworms when he really has hookworms.

Today, worming a pup is a simple matter. After examining the pup's stool, my vet sends me home with the right worm capsule, sized according to the pup's weight. Before retiring that night, I give the pup a cup of milk. First thing in the morning, the pup swallows the capsule. Two hours later, he gets his first meal of the day. A few hours later, he's free of worms.

Thereafter, spring and fall, I check him again for worms. Owners of only one dog can get by with an annual check. It's important to know your pet's weight when delivering his stool to the vet. And remember that even a dog who is free of worms will probably pick them up again if his feet touch the ground.

Aunt Tillie will probably claim that her dog never had worms. If so, he was a rarity among canines, and a golden bust of him belongs in the Smithsonian Institution.

(For the easy ways to feed capsules, pills and medicines to a dog, see SUPPLEMENTAL TIPS.)

Temperature

No matter how he looks to you, the sure sign that something is wrong with your dog is when there's more than a half degree variance either way from his normal temperature. For both dogs and cats, normal temperature is 101.2 degrees F. For a true reading, rest the dog for a half hour before taking his temperature —in a dog who has been running around it usually shoots up as high as 103 degrees F.

Temperature is always a beter indicator of health than a cold nose. A mighty sick dog can have a cold nose. The way to check is not with a family thermometer. Use a rectal thermometer, coat

15

lightly with vaseline, and insert for three minutes. The dog should be standing, even if you have to hold him up.

There's no set schedule for checking, so just use common sense. I check when I suspect that there's something wrong with a dog—and I haven't taken the temperature of some of my dogs in years.

And as it is with people, so it is with canines: there are oddball dogs and their normal temperatures are not the norm. So check your healthy puppy a few times during the first month. He may be the oddball whose normal temperature is 101 or 102.

Guardian of Canine Health

Like it or not, you are the guardian of your dog's health. Since he can't tell you when he's ill, keep your eyes open and look for these symptons: running nose or eyes, diarrhea, or traces of blood in stools for a couple of days, loss of appetite, a coat that feels dead or dry, a dog who tries to hide in dark places, or who lacks interest in the things he usually enjoys. A normal temperature, then, is not always an infallible indicator of dog health.

When a dog swallows poison, there's no time to waste. He must vomit, and he can be forced to do so by making him swallow an effective emetic. The drugstore variety of hydrogen peroxide mixed 50-50 with plain water is dandy. Figure a tablespoon for every 15 pounds of dog. Since time is so important, it's a good idea to keep a supply of the mixed formula always on hand. In a pinch, strong salt water, straight salt, or a mustard paste will do. During the action, have somebody get on the phone with the vet. If you can identify the poison or describe the dog's symptoms, he'll be able to advise as to the next step.

Many poisons are advertised as being harmless for pets, and they are left out as bait, in unprotected places, to get rid of rats and other rodents. Any vet will tell you that the poisons may not kill all dogs, but they are fatal for some. So stay away from using those "harmless" poisons.

A dog will display some or all of these symptoms when he has been poisoned: sudden paralysis, difficult breathing, excessive and often bloody diarrhea, shock, severe pain in chest or abdomen

You are the guardian of your dog's health. Since he can't tell you when he's ill, keep your eyes open for the symptoms.

HD pops up in all breeds except the Greyhound.

(yelps when you touch him), a bubbling sound from lungs, watery eyes, muscular twitching, and vomiting, Don't wait!

Hip Dysplasia (HD)

Puppy sellers, even some reliable breeders, hate to discuss HD, but it's high time that this crippling, canine affliction was brought into the open. Maybe it will save a few heartaches.

HD pops up in all breeds except the Greyhound. It is more prevalent in the big breeds (over fifty pounds), and runs rampant in some breeds, such as the German Shepherd. Despite this breed's great popularity, and maybe because of it (too many thoughtless breeders), over half the German Shepherd pups whelped in any year come down with HD.

No pup is born with HD. He develops it as he goes along, and

18

usually the symptoms aren't apparent, not even to x-ray, before a pup is six months old. HD relates to a dog's rear locomotion, or an improper fit of the femur head (rear leg) and the hip socket. The socket can be too shallow or the femur head deformed, or both. In any case, the fit is imperfect.

There are several degrees of HD, ranging from mild to severe. Mild cases are nothing to worry about. Plenty of exercise (swimming and running) builds compensating ligaments that hold the femur head in the socket. Severe cases are hopeless. The dog has trouble standing, shuffles along, and experiences severe pain. He's a real cripple, although the Harry Glumps will tell you that the dog is only suffering from arthritis, and aspirin will help.

The main cause of HD is believed to be hereditary. Insufficient nutrition during a pup's period of maximum growth (the first ten months) is another factor. Both good reasons why buying a pup from a pet store, puppy farm, mail order firm or a breeder without a reputation is always a big risk. You'll never know if the pup's sire and dam had HD or if they were started on the wrong diet. And it's a good bet that the pup's seller has never heard of HD.

Coat Care

The frequency of this home service depends upon the dog's coat: smooth, short, wiry or long. For all but the smooth coat, a metal comb is required. For all four coats, a hard bristle brush and a curry will help. Obviously, a long coat needs more attention. Otherwise, the long hairs will matt or cord, or wind themselves around a burr or a chip of wood.

It's best to start grooming a pup when he's young, whether his coat needs the care or not. This helps establish a personal relationship of trust. By the time the pup is an adult, he'll stand like a statue when you groom him. The only thing to watch is his grooming platform. For your own convenience, place him on a table, box, bench or crate. But make sure that the platform is steady. Otherwise, the pup will feel insecure and fidget.

There's only one right way to pick up a pup: one hand under his chest, the other under his rump, then hoist. Lifting a pup by his ears or tail does hurt him. And since his bones are soft, lifting

There is only one right way to pick up a pup.

him by his front legs often causes bowlegs and loose shoulders. Of course, lifting an adult Saint Bernard (165 pounds) might cause you some back trouble. If you can't teach a heavy dog to jump onto a platform, then arrange steps for him.

In coat care, the need for a comb is obvious. It should be used after a hard brushing, which loosens any dead hairs while massaging the skin. The currycomb is used to remove an abundance of hair, as when a dog is shedding. A dog is supposed to shed when the daylight hours are longest, but don't bet on it. Of all the breeds, only Bedlington Terriers and Poodles don't shed. Of the many currycombs on the market, the type I favor has a toothed blade that loops out from a leather handle.

If you live in tick country, grooming time is an excellent opportunity for finding these little monsters. The tick buries its head into the skin, sucks out blood, and his little body will blow up into the size of a nickel. The ticks have to be removed, and

20

many fainthearted owners rush their beloveds to the nearest vet for this simple operation. The easy way to remove a tick: dampen ι piece of cotton with rubbing alcohol and place cotton over tick, hen apply a little pressure with thumb and forefinger and pinch ʹt the tick. Double check to be sure you have removed the tick's ιd, since it could cause infection. The rubbing alcohol serves to nfect any slight wound. I happen to live in tick country, and ke a few minutes every day to check my dogs for ticks. (For ʹeventative measure, see SUPPLEMENTAL TIPS.)

ngroomed dogs are the ones who go through life suffering ı one or many inflictions of something as simple as dandruff to ething as unpleasant as wet or dry eczema, acne, and ring- m, or the very serious mange. Overall, grooming time is health ʔ.

ls

ny vet will tell you that about 60 per cent of the dogs in this ιtry are trotting around on poor feet. While a dog owner can astidious, he usually overlooks his pet's nails. These days, the have ceased lecturing on the subject, and most of them trim ɔg's nails without charge, even though the dogs are brought hem for other reasons.

/hen a dog trots across a wood or lineoleum floor and his feet ʹe a clicking sound, his nails are much too long. Trim back to short of the quick (nail's vein, the dark center line, easy to spot ɔod light, never runs to nail's tip.) If you hit the quick, the will bleed, but don't worry. Use a septic pencil, cold com- s, or let the dog run around on the ground. The bleeding will
.

ling the nails back is the long, hard way—and a good way to your own thumb. The easy, fast way is to use either a special nail trimmer or the more expensive electric nail trimmer. The r has a small wheel that is covered by a replaceable sand- r disk. Some breeds carry fifth toes, called dewclaws, on the ʹ of their legs. These should be trimmed, too.

he case of a pup, it's best to start trimming his nails at ten and then every three weeks or so thereafter. Since you'll

21

have both hands occupied (one to hold his paw, the other to trim the nails), you may need an assistant to hold the pup. The first few times, the average pup won't understand and will struggle. So make each session a short one and just finish two or three nails. Then try again the next day. It's not important to finish all the nails at one time. As your pup grows older and realizes that you're not going to hurt him, he'll calm down when you trim his nails. If you wait until the pup is an adult, he'll put up a real fight. The pain is very slight and only momentary. Some dogs are born tragedians, of course, and act as if they are being tortured!

Pup or dog, I put my patients on a platform. Some like to stand, and others prefer to lie on their side. Of course, there are always exceptions, and one was my yellow Labrador Retriever, Folly. She loved to have her belly rubbed, and would extend an invitation by rolling over onto her back and extending her legs. She did this as a pup and as an old lady of fifteen. So I mixed nail trimming with belly rubbing, and she was always content and cooperative.

For a long time, I had trouble with Butch, a big and very strong Samoyed. Then, purely by accident, I found that a few sips of beer turned him into a peaceful baby. Beer-drinking dogs prefer stale beer, and a half can is a great tonic for a dog who has lost his appetite. Beer is loaded with Vitamin B, an appetite stimulator.

The tonic didn't work with Boo, a bigger and stronger Bouvier des Flandres bitch. Even as a pup, Boo hated to have her nails trimmed, and she went wild whenever she saw the nail trimmer.

Diagram of a dog's nail for trimming. The dark area is the quick. Cut on dotted line.

22

After having trouble with Butch, my strong Samoyed, over cutting his nails, a few sips, taken by accident, turned him into a peaceful baby.

She weighed seventy pounds and fought like a heavyweight champion. I always needed a strong person to hold her. Nothing else upset her, and—apart from those nail-trimming sessions—she was one of the gentlest dogs in the world.

Bathing

The only rule of thumb about bathing a dog is that soap will remove the natural oils from his coat, so the frequency of baths

23

It's no disgrace if your dog has a few fleas.

should be kept to a minimum. In general, dogs keep themselves pretty clean. But they cannot attend to the interiors of their ears and can use a little help there. Use a damp cloth and mineral oil to wipe the ears out every couple of weeks.

Give your dog a bath when he's (1) obviously grubby, (2) perfuming the atmosphere with an unattractive, canine odor, or (3) supporting an army of fleas. Always use lukewarm water. Fill the bathtub to a depth of about three inches and have the dog stand in it. Use a sponge to soak his coat with the water.

The best soaps are the liquid ones designed for dogs, and the best of the lot are named Weladol and MBF. Work up a lather in your hands and then rub this lather into the coat, right down to the skin. Caution: keep soap out of eyes and ears.

After you have worked over the complete body, including the tail, drain the now dirty water from the tub. Refill with clean water and rinse the dog. If the dog has a white coat, several rinses may be necessary, although a single rinse will suffice if you use a special liquid soap called Snowy Coat. But no matter what the soap, make sure all of it is rinsed out of the coat.

Next, dry the coat with a rough towel—and keep your eye on the coat's owner for a few hours. If he runs around outdoors, he may try to roll in the nearest dirt.

About fleas: it's no disgrace if your dog has a few, because any dog can pick them up from tne ground or other dogs. So check for fleas every week. If you find some, use a flea powder or an anti-flea spray can. Then, just to be on the safe side, use either powder or spray on his bed and favorite rugs. Dog fleas are not seasonal.

Condition

A dog remains in the best of health when he's always in proper condition, and that depends on enough exercise and the right amount of daily food. A dog needs plenty of loving, too, but loving doesn't keep him in condition.

A couple of long, daily walks (half-mile) provide sufficient exercise for the small breeds, and that's why they are so desirable for city living. If you stride out, the small ones will trot.

The bigger the breed, the more exercise he needs, so a couple of long runs per day are necessary. Walking is better than nothing, but it won't help much.

Overall, the right amount of food is the big problem. Since every pup grows at his own individual rate, it is impossible to break this amount down into ounces of food per pound of puppy weight. The vital thing to remember is that any pup or adult dog should never be skinny or fat. He should always be lean, and don't let Aunt Tillie lead you astray on that point.

A lean dog's flesh just covers his rib cage. If you can see a pup's ribs, he needs a little more food each day. If the pup has a long coat, use your fingers to determine his condition.

A couple of long, daily walks are sufficient for the small breeds. A couple of long runs per day are necessary for the big dogs.

Obviously, a skinny pup will be under par, lacking in energy, and open to all sorts of diseases and infections. A fat pup carries too much weight for his growing. Since any growing puppy's bones are always soft, it's idiotic to keep the young animal fat (overweight). Also, one of the big dangers is that he can develop HD. Because of canine anatomy, a dog's hips are always under more stress than his shoulders. His hips are his power plant, and they must be kept in working order.

In the hope of selling more dog food, some of the big companies recommend that their foods be kept available for dogs at all times. In other words, let the dog eat as much as he wants whenever he wants. This advice may appeal to lazy owners, but it's dangerous for their dogs. The average cat won't overeat, but the average dog will stuff himself until he can't stand.

Any pup goes through his maximum period of growth in his first ten months. All during that time, he requires about twice as much food per day as he will as an adult. His digestive juices, however, cannot handle all that at one time, so he should be fed several times a day. This is also a convenience for his owner. If a pup looks too thin, make one meal bigger. If he becomes fat, cut down on one meal. Check his condition every few days and make sure that he stays lean.

Feeding Schedule

You'll find all sorts of advice about the number of times to feed a pup per day, but here's the schedule I've found to be the very best:

6 to 10 weeks—4 times
10 weeks to 4 months—3 times
4 months to 8 months—2 times

Along about the seventh month, cut down the quantity of both meals. At eight months, start feeding one meal, and let leanness be your guide as to quantity. If you feed in the morning, give him a dog biscuit in the afternoon, just to keep him happy.

At twelve months, the pup becomes an adult, and the size of his one meal per day remains pretty constant for the rest of his life. If he's a housedog, then he no longer gets a biscuit. If he's a kennel dog, I give him a biscuit, but only in winter. This seems fair, since my house dogs lick the dinner plates and the pots and pans.

The Right Food

Prepared dog food is now close to a billion-dollar business in this country, and there are more than 2,500 national, regional, and local companies in the act. So competition is hot. A great deal of the advertising is misleading, and, thus far, the companies have

Your dog needs carbohydrates, proteins, fat, certain vitamins and minerals, and plenty of water.

enjoyed freedom from control.

Canned (wet) and dry (meal and kibble) are the two popular types of food found in any grocery store or supermarket. Every brand of food is promoted as being all that your dog needs to eat, but such is not the case. "Your dog must have meat" is a totally invalid claim. Too often, so is "Balanced nutritional diet."

Just what nutrients does your dog require for growth, health and longevity? He needs carbohydrates, proteins, fat, certain vitamins and minerals, and plenty of water.

According to their labels, many of the canned brands do meet and often exceed the nutritional canine requirements of the National Research Council. Since all boast of more than 50 per cent moisture, they do help meet the dog's water requirements, but water from the tap is much cheaper. And while the protein count might be right for an adult dog, a growing pup needs twice as much protein. Furthermore, no brand promises that the protein and vitamins are digestible. And do any of the companies know that too much Vitamin A will stunt a pup's growth? Apparently not. And what about meat and meat byproducts? Some of the byproducts make fine filler, but they are worthless as nutrients.

I know of no veterinarian who believes that any of the canned foods, in themselves, constitute a proper canine diet. I do not know a single veteran breeder who feeds canned foods exclusively. On the other hand, I know of many large, successful kennels where meat (canned or fresh) has not been fed in years.

One of the great myths of our time is that a dog needs meat because he is a carniverous animal. The manufacturers of canned foods are happy to perpetuate this myth, although the dog, after thousands of years of domestication, is now almost as omnivorous an animal as you are. Except for raw starches, his digestive tract is just as good as yours. And you really don't need meat, as all nutritionists, vegetarians—and bulls—will attest.

It is true that meat is a source of protein, fat, and calcium phosphate. But the protein count isn't much, and there are far cheaper and better sources for fats. Also, meat has a laxative effect on some dogs. And now, thanks to recent research, we know that what a dog needs is calcium lactate, as found in milk, solid or powdered. His mineral and vitamins needs are minimal, and he finds enough of both in almost any food you offer him. Since unneeded vitamins and minerals pass right through a dog, the expensive food supplements are usually a waste of money. Use them only at your vet's suggestion. Sometimes they are of benefit to older dogs.

A quality dry food (kibble), one with a label reading at least 22 per cent protein and 6 per cent fat, is always a better health bet than the canned foods. The dry brands usually come in 25- and 50-pound bags and should be stored in a dry place.

I happen to buy my dried food in 300-pound lots and store the bags in metal garbage cans. The cans keep out moisture, mice and rats. The only thing to watch with a quantity of dry food is the site where it is stored. It should not be a hot place, since mealy worms might result.

To make it easier to digest, dry kibble is soaked for about fifteen minutes. For a 60-pound Labrador, I use about four heaping cups of kibble. The kibble goes into the dog's dish and is just covered with water or some other liquid, such as sour milk or the water saved from cooking vegetables. Once the kibble is soaked, I add a couple of tablespoonfuls of canned fish (jack mackerel) for flavor and additional protein. Twice a week, I add one hard boiled egg (a raw egg will cause diarrhea), just to be sure about protein, and a handful of chopped suet or a tablespoonful of fat saved from a roast or bacon, just to be sure about enough fat. A growing pup gets a hard boiled egg every other day.

That diet keeps my dogs in great condition. A couple of them think it isn't enough, however. For them, I add leftover cooked vegetables, which give them more minerals and vitamins, but won't add any poundage to their frames.

A little caution about vegetables: just about anything you eat, except members of the cabbage family—and go easy on the cooked starches (corn, potatoes, rice, etc.). And any fruit you like is fine for your dog.

And a little advice to the meat diehards: if you can't cure loose stools or diarrhea, substitute canned chicken (the cheapest brand available) or canned fish.

Your Dog's Veterinarian

One of our country's acute shortages is the supply of practicing veterinarians. The U.S.A. has only eighteen veterinary colleges, whose graduates total fewer than 1,000 each year. Half of these go into federal, industrial, business research, and public health jobs. The others hope to hang out their own shingles some day, but most join the staffs of existing small animal hospitals. Since it takes a young fortune in equipment to get going (about $40,000), very few new vets can afford to go into private practice.

30

There is a shortage of veterinarians, so all of them are extremely busy.

In view of the shortage—and it will get worse as the pet population continues to explode—locating the right vet for your dog or dogs is no longer a simple matter. All the vets are extremely busy. If an emergency occurred this minute and you phoned a veterinarian who does not know you, chances are that you would have to settle for an appointment several days from now. Meanwhile, your pet might die.

So don't wait for an emergency. Even before you bring your pup home, check around with other dog owners, breeders, and even cat lovers. Find the name of the local veterinarian most of them favor. The best vet in town may not charge more than the worst one in the country. As soon as possible, make an appointment for the pup's permanent shots. If you like the doctor, either him or her, try to become more than a client. He'll be too busy to come to dinner, but you can always send him birthday and Xmas cards.

Many veterinarians limit their business to small animal pets and birds, such as dogs, cats, canaries and finches. That's almost always true in the city, where pet cows are seldom found. But if you don't live in the city, then you often have a choice between a small animal vet and the complete vet; that is, the man who takes care of both pets and livestock. Given a choice, I always vote for the latter. Whenever I move, I make it a point to check out the local vets with farmers as well as dog breeders. Sometimes, what works for a horse will work for a dog. And a vet who is used to staying up all night with a sick calf doesn't mind being called at four in the morning.

So if you own a pup right now and don't have a regular vet, you are living dangerously.

Judging from my own mail, young ladies are the people most concerned about canine safety. All dog lovers should be, for the annual toll of avoidable canine deaths is almost unbelievable. The real tragedy lies in the fact that millions of intelligent Americans are irresponsible pet owners. Let's look at a few annual statistics:

1. Dogs killed on highways and streets: about three million. Many pups regard rolling trucks as friends. Many adult dogs think

Somewhere around nine million pet dogs are killed in one year!

that they can outrun speeding vehicles. At night and in stormy weather, dogs and drivers can't see each other coming.

2. Dogs stolen by professionals: about two million. The professionals are known as bunchers, in that they cruise residential areas, pick up friendly dogs until they have a bunch of them, then ship the bunch to another state within twenty-four hours. The dogs are sold to a holding farm and the farm resells them at a profit to research laboratories. Many of these laboratories receive federal funds. While there are exceptions (Brookhaven is one of them), a dog doesn't last very long in the average lab.

3. Dogs stolen by amateurs: over one million. Most of the amateurs call themselves sportsmen, since they hunt. They steal dogs of the sporting and hound breeds for use during the hunting season. If a dog doesn't work out, he is shot and another is stolen. At season's end, the hunting dogs are shot or abandoned. Many of the latter starve or are killed in accidents.

4. Killed by dog haters: over one million. There are as many dog haters as there are dog lovers, and some of the haters have short tempers. They value their lawns, shrubs, gardens and garbage cans more than they do your dog's life. Guns and poisons represent their short tempers.

5. Killed by the careless: about two million. Some hunters shoot at anything that moves, including dogs, cats, and people, and we have more than thirty million hunters. The nicest man in town backs his car out of the garage, not realizing that his neighbor's dog is sleeping on the driveway. Trappers find dogs in their traps, shoot them, then reset the traps. And nobody told the painter not to leave the open cans of paint on the porch when he went to lunch; he assumed the puppy wouldn't drink the paint and die of lead poisoning.

Somewhere around nine million pet dogs killed in one year! Hard to believe, isn't it? Still, those are the best estimates available, and even if they are off by several thousands, the hard fact remains that millions of owners committed one simple sin: each permitted his dog to run free.

"It just isn't right to coop up a dog" is a phrase that one hears much too often, and I would like to find a way to make its utterance illegal. It may have made a little sense a hundred years ago, but today we have too many vehicles, hunters are wilder than ever, and dog stealing is big business. Despite the fact that leash laws now exist in many communities, and hundreds of more communities will adopt them over the coming years, so far, the laws have not proved very effective. The average leash law specifies that a dog cannot be off his owner's property unless he is under control on a leash. The trouble is that there aren't enough dog wardens and policemen around to enforce the laws. When an owner is hauled into court, he still refuses to recognize his responsibility. "I told Bozo not to leave the front yard," is a common plea. Usually, Bozo hasn't been trained to obey.

In many rural communities, the law states that a dog can be shot if he is found off his owner's property between sundown and sunup. Again, most dog owners have remained unimpressed. They assume that, when they "kick the dog out for the night," the animal will stick around. Also, they know that the sheriff is too busy to hunt for loose dogs. When they learn that their dogs have been killed on a highway two miles from home, they blame hit-and-run drivers.

Obviously, it doesn't make much sense to buy a pup, raise him, love him, and train him—and then let him run free. For heaven's sake, make sure that you know where your dog is all of the time. That's never a problem, of course, when he's indoors, or when you're outdoors with him and have him under control. But unless you have a high (six-foot) fence around your yard and the gates are always secure, don't trust even a well-trained dog to stay on the home grounds when he's not supervised. The sight of a cat or another dog across the street may lure him away. Any male dog over eight months will scent a bitch in season a mile away, and he will not be able to resist the temptation to trot off and find romance, although he'll probably end up in a dog fight.

If you have the square footage, the obvious answer to the big outdoor problem is a dog run. This is a safe place to park your pet when you're in school and your mother wants to clean the house, or when you just want him out of the way—as when friends who are afraid of dogs pay a visit. (For how to build a simple, practical,

35

inexpensive outdoor run, see INSIDE INFORMATION.)

Beyond responsibility, the nitty-gritty of dog ownership is really dog training. While a dog of any age can be trained, the younger he is started, the easier it is for his teacher. The pup is finding out about life, has not developed any personal habits, and is ripe for learning things your way. An untrained, adult dog is operating at his maximum degree of intelligence, possesses firm habits, and has definite ideas about his style of life. Training at an older age takes a great deal more time and patience.

Since most dogs come to their new homes as pups, the training methods herein relate to the younger generation, although they can be applied to a dog of any age. It is never too late, for example, to rename a dog and train him to respond to his new name.

It always amazes me that a mother who has raised seven model children encounters all sorts of problems when she tries to train a pup. Even naming a pup is sometimes a puzzler, and I've spent too many hours explaining that a pup who has been registered by his breeder with the American Kennel Club as Archibald Shadow of Zoola does not have to carry that name throughout his life. The pup doesn't know his name and would prefer, if granted a say in the matter, something much simpler.

Overall, the naming and training of any pup should be simple matters and never problems. Please don't write! I'm not a grumpy old man, but I am a little weary of offering these simple solutions to perplexed new puppy owners, many of them college graduates. Let's examine the most pressing dog training problems of our time in logical sequence:

Naming

Before bringing the new pup home, predetermine his pet name. Announce his name to other members of the family and request that they abide by your decision. After you have picked up your pup and are on the way home, talk to him and use his name frequently. Carry him on your lap. For your own safety, or just in case, spread an old towel over your lap or wrap it around him.

Ideally, the pup's name should be short—just one or two syllables. While length doesn't matter to him, a short name is healthier for you. Shout a name like Archibald into the wind for a half hour and you'll become hoarse. The name Archy would be easier on your vocal cords.

Ever since the first canine authority was recognized, all the other authorities have insisted that the pet name should not conflict with a command word. Thus, Sid is considered a poor choice, since it sounds like the command "Sit!" But if you speak clearly and don't slur your words, Sid is a fine name. The canine ear is a remarkably sensitive instrument.

Consider the case of my friend Brookie, a dog owned by another friend, Chan Tenney. As a pup, Brookie was taught how to spell, in the sense that he was trained to obey a command word only when that command word was spelled correctly. Brookie is an old man now, but he still won't fetch an object if Chan says, "F-E-T-S-H" or "F-E-C-T-H" or any other misspelling of the command word.

Believe this: no matter what name you select, so long as you stick to that one name and use it frequently, as when you're petting and talking to the pup, he'll learn the name is his in just a few days.

The canine associates almost everything with sound or movement. The more he hears the sound of his name, the sooner he learns it.

Housebreaking

This is just a matter of getting the pup outdoors (or onto paper, if he's to be paper trained) at the critical times, and those times occur with great frequency.

A pup plays, drinks, eats and does a lot of sleeping. He is a baby, doesn't wear diapers, and responds to the calls of nature in automatic fashion. He learns the sanitary rules of society by habit, and the habit must be imposed by you, or by somebody else in your absence.

These are the critical times when you should take the pup outdoors:

1. After every nap or long sleep.
2. After every indoor play session.

3. Before and after he dines or drinks.

4. When he awakens in the morning, and just before he goes to sleep at night. It helps him if you remove his drinking water several hours before you plan to retire.

5. Whenever he exhibits telltale signs, such as circling or sniffing a spot, going to the door, or whining.

If you remain on the alert, your pup will be housebroken in just a few days. Rain or shine, get him outdoors fast at the critical times, and at all other times when you think he's about to relieve himself. If it is raining and he gets soaking wet, rub him dry when he comes back into the house.

Now, there are going to be critical times when you rush him outdoors and nothing happens. Just be patient. It will.

The only other thing to watch is your own deportment. Punishment—even a scolding tone of voice—won't mean a thing to the very young puppy if he does have an accident. He won't understand because he doesn't have the brains to understand. You'll only confuse him by reprimanding him.

Once housebroken, he'll still need to get outdoors at the critical times. He may alert you by standing at the door or whining, and he may not. And—unless you were born under a lucky star—he will have an indoor accident now and again over the next few months, usually because you've been lazy or haven't been watching him. After he's four months old, the average pup needs to get outdoors every two hours. By then, he'll be old and wise enough to be able to relate a scolding to punishment.

He'll also be old enough to take a prompt mild whack over the hindquarters as punishment for something wrong he has just done. Whacking him ten minutes later won't mean a thing. For the purpose, the palm of the hand is sufficient. A rolled newspaper will do, of course, but it takes time to find and roll a newspaper. One's hand is handier.

Collar and Leash

There's a huge variety of collars. Most are designed for eye appeal (*your* eye), and they are both overpriced and impractical. As puppy or adult, the average dog doesn't really need a thick

*A simple slip collar, made of nylon
cord, is very satisfactory.*

leather collar or a length of big link chain around his neck. On long-coated breeds, of course, both types help ruin the coat.

A simple slip collar is very satisfactory, and the best and most economical around are made of soft, nylon cord. The collar comes in a variety of colors and is washable. It's just a length of cord with a metal ring attached to each end. When pushed through one ring, a loop is created, and the loop becomes the collar. For the right fit, the loop should just be large enough to pass over the pup's head and ears. The slip collar hangs loosely around the neck, and the leash is attached to the free ring. Yank on this ring and the collar tightens—as when a panicky puppy tries to back out of the confining circlet.

An added, unadvertised feature of this nylon slip collar is safety. If the collar catches on anything, the pup can either pull it over his head or chew his way through it. The only real drawback is that a puppy-size collar won't be big enough for him as an adult dog, but these collars are still priced around one dollar.

Only the exceptional puppy doesn't resent a collar around his neck. Over the first few days, let him wear it for periods of five minutes several times a day. Play with him so that his attention will be distracted. In about four days, he won't notice the collar and you can leave it on him at all times.

As for the leash, the most practical and economical one around is made of webbed canvas. When the pup gets used to his collar, attach the leash to the right ring, and let him drag it around and play with it. Again, short sessions, several times a day. On the third or fourth day, take him for a couple of short walks on leash, but let him do the leading. The big idea is to get him on friendly terms with the leash, so that he won't fight it later on.

When the pup knows his name and is housebroken, and after he gets accustomed to his collar and leash, he's ready to learn the first of several basic commands that will turn him into an obedient pet. Like it or lump it, you should be the dog's only trainer. He'll be confused if every member of your family and close friends get into the act. From the start, you are the sole boss. It doesn't make any difference whether you train him indoors or out, or what

The dog who heels properly stays at your left side when you want him there, whether you are standing, walking, or running.

sequence you use in teaching the commands, but there are a few, helpful basics:

1. The fewer the distractions, the easier the training. Having friends present won't help.

2. Use your natural tone of voice. Keep it pleasant, but firm. A shout is a roar to a pup, and it might frighten him.

3. Keep training sessions short, and quit when the pup gets bored. His attention span is limited, and training should be fun for him. Reward a good job with praise or a tidbit, and always play with him after each training period. You're his friend, not his enemy.

4. The slip collar and leash are the best training tools. A little yank on the leash will tighten the collar. The pup will feel it, but it won't hurt him. Use the yank as a corrective measure.

5. Don't rush the training. One command at a time. Once started, a puppy catches on fast. If he learns his first command in a week, he'll learn his third command in about four days.

6. It helps if you use his name before giving the command word, as in "Duke, heel!" Then the pup knows you are talking to him, and not to the sparrow he's watching. Try not to run the two words together. Make it: "Duke (pause), heel!"

One more thing: it's useless to teach a command unless you continue to use it. Train a pup to sit, then neglect to tell him to sit for a month, and chances are that he'll forget those earlier lessons. So, once you've trained a dog to do something, refresh his memory (at your convenience) every day or so. An adult has a memory bank, but not a pup.

Please believe two things: I've trained many pups, and I'm a lazy man. So I do things the easy way, and here's my system:

"Heel!"

The dog who heels properly stays at your left side when you want him there, whether you are just standing or else walking or running. It keeps a pup safe in some situations, as when you're crossing a busy highway with him. After he learns the command, it doesn't make much difference whether he stays at your left or right side, and sometimes it helps to have him switch sides, as

As you say, "Duke, sit!" yank up on the leash and press down on the pup's hindquarters with your left hand.

when you're trying to find a path through a crowd.

In the beginning, it's always best for most owners to start the pup on the left. Why? The puppy already regards your right hand as a kindly thing: it feeds him and pets him. So you correct with your left hand. Of course, if you happen to be left-handed, just reverse the following advice: Hold your end of the leash in your right hand, run it across the front of your body, and grasp it with the left hand. The leash runs from your right hand to your left hand and then to the pup's collar.

Your left hand is the control point. Use this hand to yank on the leash whenever the pup lags or tries to dash off. Sooner or later, he's going to realize that, when he stays at your left side, his collar won't tighten.

Place the pup on your left, say, "Duke, heel!" and start walking. With every yank, repeat, "Duke, heel!" If he stays at your side for only five seconds, be sure to praise him.

If the weather is fair, I usually take a couple of brief walks in the woods every day, and I take a pup along. I keep him on leash for about four minutes, then let him run free for awhile. Then I put him back on leash when we're about three minutes from home. With this system, the average pup heels off leash on the fifth day.

"Sit!"

For this command, your right hand is the control point. Face the pup and have him standing. Hold the leash short.

As you say, "Duke, sit!" yank up on the leash and press down on the pup's hindquarters with your left hand. He'll sit. Sometimes, a pup will learn to sit on command in just one training session. The average pup needs about twenty minutes, spread over two days. Note that both hands are doing the correcting. To reassure your dog, pet him with your kindly right hand as soon as he sits.

"Stay!"

This is a very important command, since it can be taught two ways and simultaneously: verbal and hand signal. The hand signal has saved the life of many dogs, because the pup who knows what it means stays where he is. When your pup can't

Give the "Duke, stay!" command and swing the palm of your left hand toward his nose.

hear your voice because of heavy traffic, and he's about to dash across the street to join you, he'll see the hand signal and stop.

Have the pup sitting at your left side, without his leash attached. As you step off, give the "Duke, stay!" command, and swing the palm of your left hand toward his nose. If the pup moves, and he probably will, grab him with your left hand, have him sit, and try again.

I like to call this a gradual command, because a frisky pup is bound to break after you get a few feet away. So success comes gradually: five feet, ten feet, and finally twenty. Any pup who learns this command in three days is a canine genius.

He's a canine Einstein if, after a couple of weeks, he will sit on command when you're twenty feet away and then stay there on command. When he sits, face him, and use the hand signal with the stay command. At a distance, you can use either hand for the hand signal. Just arc the arm up and toward him from your side, with the palm of your hand toward him.

"Down!"

When your pup will sit and stay on command, teaching him to go down is a cinch. For this command, it's back to the leash again, and your right foot is the control point.

Tell the pup to sit and stay. Face him, straight on, with the leash looped from your right hand to his collar. The middle of the loop should be about three inches above ground level.

As you give the command "Duke, down!" step on the loop. The pressure will bring the pup down, but it won't hurt him. Repeat, and be lavish with your praise after each repeat. A bright pup learns this command in a hurry, often in one day.

"Come!"

This is a command many pups don't have to learn. As soon as they hear their names, they come on the double. But many other puppies aren't that cooperative, and they require training.

The training can start indoors on a rainy day. With the pup on leash, put him on a sit and stay and face him. Hold the leash in your right hand, and give a yank as you say, "Duke, come!" If he

46

As you give the command "Duke, down!" step on the loop.

doesn't come, haul him to you.

Constant repetition is the key to success. After a pup responds without the yank, it's time to increase the distance between you.

The big danger in teaching this command is overconfidence on the part of the trainer. Often a pup who will respond perfectly (off leash) at ten feet won't do so at thirty. Indeed, at any distance over ten feet, he's likely to run in the other direction.

Chasing him isn't the answer. He must come to you. Just keep repeating the command and invent some way to attract him: clap your hands, roll on the ground, stand on your head, or run in the opposite direction. Eventually, the pup will come to you. Whether this takes three minutes or a half hour, keep cool and don't discipline him when he finally comes to you. Although delinquent, the pup has done his job. If you reprimand him, he may decide not to answer your command the next time. So be lavish with your congratulations, or you'll damage the training program.

A pup off leash who won't respond to your antics must go back to the leash. Tie a rope to your end of the leash, thus increasing length, and repeat the first lessons. Depending on your pet, this can be the easiest or the most difficult command to teach. It takes all kinds of pups to make the world.

Heel, sit, stay, down, and come—for your convenience and his, those are the commands every dog should know. But don't expect him to be perfect every time. He'll improve as he matures.

Ideally, you should be the sole trainer of your pup, but that's often impractical. Obviously, other members of the family may try to get into the act from time to time, as when you are absent. So it's always best to have a meeting of the minds and make sure that all parties train in the same manner. If your family is a reasonable one, that shouldn't be difficult.

If you insist on teaching tricks, don't muddle the pup's mind before he has his basic commands down pat, more or less. Important things first.

Teaching any trick is merely a matter of leading a dog through the desired motions and rewarding him in a generous fashion. Repetition is the key to success. I don't teach even simple tricks to my dogs, since most serve no practical purpose, and offend

Eventually, the pup will come to you. Whether this takes three minutes or half an hour, keep cool.

If you insist on teaching tricks, don't muddle the pup's mind before he has his basic commands down pat.

canine dignity. Trick performing dogs remind me of children whose mothers insist that they play the piano or recite poetry when company arrives, often to the distress of the company. However, to each his own.

I derive my own kicks from studying a puppy as he matures, learns, and begins to develop the traits that will establish him as an individual personality. Hardly anything is known about these traits, but my hunch is that some are inherited. My dog Thumper, for example, is a third generation greeter. Like his sire and grandsire, he always presents a gift to anyone who enters the house. He grabs whatever is handy and trots to the door with his jaws full of shoes, a book, or letters from a wastebasket. Lass, his daughter, always jumps up on me when my back is turned. Her dam did that, too. But Thumper's dam, Folly, is the only dog we've ever owned who stole napkins from the laps of dinner guests. She did this without anybody noticing, but we always knew where to look for the napkins. They were always tucked away under the same

50

bed. David, Folly's grandson, is coming along as a thief, but he still lacks her professional touch. His specialty is stealing food from an unattended counter or table.

Up to this point, we've been dealing with questions more or less related with puppyhood. There are all sorts of other interesting things to know about a pup, but none are too important. He starts losing his puppy (milk) teeth between his fourth and fifth months of age, for example, as they are replaced by his permanent teeth. The transition period covers about three weeks, and during

I don't teach even simple tricks to my dogs, since most serve no practical purpose and offend canine dignity.

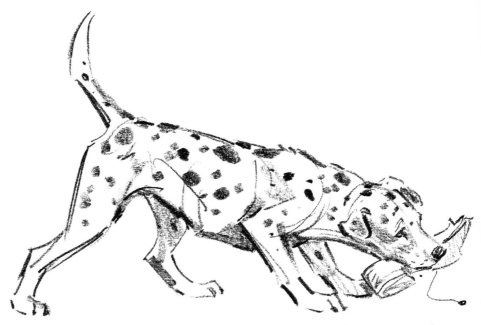

Like his sire and grandsire, he always presents a gift to anyone who enters the house.

this time the pup gets a little edgy, so any training should be on the light side. The mystery of the lost puppy teeth is that one seldom finds them. They seem to disappear into thin air. Maybe the pup swallows them. I've raised scores of pups and found fewer than a dozen lost teeth.

Now let's deal with some questions that pertain to dogs of all ages. For a starter, here's one that also involves canine teeth:

My vet told me not to give bones to my dog, but my friends tell me I'm foolish. What's wrong with bones?

Tell Tom, Dick, and Harry to jump in the lake. Your vet is correct. Bones can (1) break teeth, (2) splinter and strangle your dog, and (3) splinter and pierce the lining of the stomach.

If you insist on feeding bones, and many owners do, confine the canine treats to the mildly dangerous knuckle bones, and take a vow never, never to feed the very dangerous splintery chicken bones. Fortunately, there are several artificial bones now on the

David's specialty is stealing food from an unattended table.

market that are safe substitutes for the real things and absolutely harmless. The best of the lot is called Nylabone. The rawhide bones are also harmless, but they don't last very long. Both types are great for pups during the teething stage, when they will chew anything within reach of their jaws and love to damage chair legs, new shoes, and corners of rugs. For older dogs, both kinds help keep the teeth free from tartar. These bones are not expensive.

My three-year-old Dalmatian has been much too thin for about five months, and I can't put weight on him. What foods are weight builders?

Your dog probably has tapeworms, whipworms, or both. Check him out. If he's worm free, cut one-third of his daily ration and substitute (same weight) either cooked spaghetti or cooked rice. Both are starches, and both will add pounds. A dog's digestive juices can't handle raw starches.

I have a dog who won't get his feet wet, much less swim. Aren't all dogs supposed to be swimmers?

Any dog is capable of swimming, and some breeds love the water more than others. But any normal person is capable of swimming, and many people won't go near the water. For both dogs and people, the problem is fear, or a feeling of aquatic insecurity.

The worst thing to do is the most obvious: toss the dog into deep water. He'll swim for his life all right, but his fear will increase.

My own training tool for teaching a dog to swim is a small boat fender. This is about a foot long, covered with canvas, and stuffed with cork. It floats.

I toss this bumper over dry land and teach the dog to retrieve it. Most dogs love this game, and after a week they'll go after the bumper in water, gradually venturing deeper and deeper until, finally, they will go leaping into water so deep that they have to swim a little for it. Easy stages solve the problem.

On leash, some dogs will walk in shallow water with their

Some breeds love the water more than others.

owners. Keep such a dog at heel, and increase the depth of the water each time out.

A small dog, no matter what his age, can be carried into water over his depth. He'll cling, and the idea is to keep reassuring him. Do this several times a day for about three days before releasing him gently in the water. When you do, wade for shore and he'll swim after you. Repeat a few times for another three days and the dog will overcome his fear of water and become a swimming fool. It's easier to teach a dog to swim than a cat.

Do any of the wild animals make better pets than dogs?

It has been proved that a wild animal, no matter how young and sweet, will revert to his wild, inherited instincts as an adult. Also, to capture the young ones, pet store suppliers must almost always shoot the mothers. Forget the wild ones and don't keep the inhumane suppliers in business. It took a few thousand years, by the way, to domesticate the canine. You can hardly expect to domesticate a wild animal in just one generation or two. The ocelot, as an example, is still being promoted as a perfect pet. Admire his beauty but not his instincts. Before he's two years old, this cat spells trouble. Ask your veterinarian.

I know that the Chesapeake Bay Retriever was developed in this country. Are there any other All American breeds?

Five more: Boston Terrier, American Foxhound, Alaskan Malamute, American Water Spaniel, and Black and Tan Coonhound. Of these six, the Chesapeake and the Boston are the best pet breeds for young dog lovers. Since he's smaller and his smooth coat requires less grooming, the Boston is the best bet for city dwellers. Forty years ago, this was the most popular breed around. Today, the Boston ranks about twentieth and the Chessie is forty-ninth. Any breed's popularity goes up and down every few years for no apparent reasons.

My dog is fascinated by skunks, but they never appreciate his overtures, and I spend a young fortune on tomato juice every year. How do you cure a dog of his liking for skunks?

Once is enough for most dogs. In your case, try letting him live with the unpleasant odor for a few days—if you can keep him penned far enough away from the house. Or, if you feel you must wash him, scold him and let him know you're unhappy as you go about the unpleasant task. A dog is often sensitive to his master's mood, and he might associate your unhappiness with his recent adventure. Worth a try.

Tomato juice is not the best choice for ridding a dog of skunk perfume. Follow the directions outlined previously for bathing a dog, but use water a little hotter than lukewarm. Numerous

*Take a little time to introduce your
dog personally to the mailman.*

resent something irresistible to him. A couple of methods that work sometimes:

1. Enlist the help of two friends who will drive past your house at slow speed and shoot blank cartridges or water pistols at the chasing dog. Repeat over a period of several days.

2. Have your friends stop the car, hop out, and chase your dog, shouting as they do so. If they catch him, they should scold him and whack him over the quarters with rolled newspaper. Once is usually enough.

The above also applies to dogs who chase bicycle riders, horseback riders, and motorcycles.

If there's a cat in the family, a dog seldom chases other people's cats. But even a cat-loving dog will often make things hard on a mailman. The man represents an intruder. Take a little time to introduce your dog personally to the mailman, let him know the man is a friend, and that's the end of that problem.

My dog Thumper was seven when I moved to my present homestead. It is located at the end of a long, lonely road in a forest, and it's the last place the snowplow reaches. The first winter, Thumper decided to chase the snowplow.

If it had been possible to bring the snowplow into the house, the plow and the dog would have become friends, and the problem would have been solved. Since that was impractical, I invited the plowmen into the house to have coffee. They did this after every snowstorm and became Thumper's friends. He would watch them climb into the cab and drive off, and he stopped chasing the snowplow.

Now, four winters later, Thumper still doesn't chase the plow, although the plowmen are different people, and don't like to rest and have coffee. So the dog doesn't know the two men, but he thinks he does. The canine's limited intelligence (compared to that of humans) works to my advantage.

Why isn't Thumper in an outdoor run? Well, he's a house dog, but he must go outdoors every so often. In winter, the only traffic is the plow and the mailman. In other seasons, only the mailman, who arrives by car. The law insists that I have a mailbox, so I have one, but it is seldom used. At noon each day, Thumper waits at the end of the drive, accepts the mail, and carries it back to the house in his jaws. It was his idea. The mailman, his friend, is very cooperative.

We are looking for a good watchdog. What is the best breed for the purpose?

Any dog who will bark at strangers makes a good watchdog, so breed and size don't matter. His bark should alert you.

For heaven's sake, don't buy or train a dog to attack. Almost everywhere in this country, the law is on the side of the damaged person. You can have a man arrested if he robs you, but if your dog bites him, on or off your property, when he comes to rob, he can sue you.

I live on a small farm and have plenty of room for dogs. To earn extra money, I would like to go into breeding, and am anxious to start the right way with a quality bitch. My parents approve, but we are not able to pay a high price. My heart is set on your breed, the Labrador Retriever. Do you ever have free pups?

"The best things in life are free" does not work in the dog game, and most breeders will agree with me. I learned my lesson years ago, when I gave several free pups to friends and relatives. None of the pups received proper care.

Human nature is funny. If a human doesn't invest in something, he doesn't appreciate it. No matter what the value of a gift, the beneficiary usually feels no great personal loss when it is destroyed.

In your case, you seem willing to invest time and care, so shortage of cash is not a great problem. (See INSIDE INFORMATION.)

How does one remove porcupine quills from a dog?

This is tricky. If you haven't had any experience and the penetrations are deep, your vet is the man to handle the removals.

If the vet isn't immediately available, then the removal is up to you. The longer you wait, the deeper the quills will penetrate, for a dog won't remain still and will try to rub against something. He's hurting.

61

My method of removing quills was taught to me by my father. It always worked for him and it has always worked for me, but it differs from any advice I've ever read. Perhaps the advice-givers haven't had any practical experience. We are in agreement on just one thing: the penetrating end of the quill is covered with tiny barbs.

First, I find the angle of the quill's penetration. Then I grasp the quill close to the dog's skin with thumb and forefinger, push up or down in the direction of the angle (thus releasing the deepest set barbs), and pull out quickly at the same angle. Sometimes the quill goes right through the lips and tongue. In that case, snip off the quill at barbed end and pull the rest of the quill on through.

The deeper the penetration, the more the blood. Have an antiseptic handy to treat each wound. Rubbing alcohol is fine. Use cotton to dab it on the wound. While the penetration of the quills on the body of a long-coated dog is never deep, the quills themselves are sometimes easy to miss. So inspect carefully and make sure you get every quill. In my experience, quills are either light yellow or light gray. However, I keep reading that porky's quills are always black. Maybe I need new glasses.

The porcupine does not "shoot" his quills. He releases them by brushing against the dog, and his tail does most of the damage. Porky uses it in self-defense, as a man would use a club. Since he doesn't go looking for trouble, blame your dog for being too inquisitive at the wrong time. Obviously, you may need somebody to hold your dog during the quill-removing operation. And if the quills are set deep into his body, tie a length of rag around his muzzle, just in case the pain makes him angry.

Sometimes my dog comes home smelling pretty awful. He likes to roll in manure piles or anything else that smells terrible. Why does he do this and how do I cure him?

This is called atavism, or a reversion to an ancient instinct of your dog's wild ancestors. The wild ones were hunters, of course, and they disguised their own scent by rolling in stronger ones. Thus, they were able to ambush their wary prey. The wild hare didn't realize that he was hopping into the jaws of a dog, because

62

In the end, my Labrador wouldn't even look at a guppy swimming in a tank.

the dog smelled like an elephant, and the hare wasn't afraid of an elephant.

Well, that's the popular theory, but I find it difficult to buy. If true, the wild dog was far more intelligent than the domestic dog, and thousands of years of canine development have gone down the drain.

My personal theory is that some dogs are as odd as some people, and it takes all kinds to make a world. Consider the people who think the scent of Limburger cheese is delightful.

The sure cure for your dog, of course, is not to let him run free. If you can't be convinced of that, check the advice given for skunk chasers.

Years ago, when I lived along the shore, a Lab of mine started rolling on the decaying bodies of dead fish. I tied a smelly, dead fish around his neck and confined him to an outdoor run. This didn't work an immediate cure, but I repeated it about three times, and, in the end, the dog, wouldn't even look at a guppy swimming in a tank.

My teacher owns a Poodle and she claims that this is really a sporting breed. I'd say her little dog would be frightened by a rabbit. So?

Your teacher has her breed history down pat, but not her varieties. The Standard Poodle (over fifteen inches) was originally developed in Germany to retrieve game birds from water. The Toy (up to ten inches) and the Miniature (just over ten inches and up to fifteen inches) varieties were developed to serve only as pets. These days, very few Standards are used for their original purpose. There are better retriever breeds around.

There are more Miniatures than Toys in the United States and more Toys than Standards. Added together, the three varieties make the Poodle the most popular breed (by far) in the U.S.A. Currently, better than 25 per cent of the purebred pups whelped in this country are Poodles, and this percentage should hold up for many years to come. Whatever his size, the average Poodle is an extremely intelligent dog.

Whether you ever own a Poodle or not, it's possible for you

64

to profit from the breed's popularity and put money into the bank. (Check out in INSIDE INFORMATION.)

I have an outdoor run and house for my dog. Does hay or straw make the best bedding?

Both straw and hay make inferior bedding. While both are absorbent, they retain moisture and dry slowly. Also, both provide dust that works into a dog's coat and can irritate the eyes and nostrils. And both are fine hiding places for fleas.

Cedar ribbons (not chips) make the best bedding. They are hard to find in some sections of the country, and usually expensive at pet stores. The best sources are feed stores and lumber yards. The cedar ribbons have these advantages: (1) absorbent, but quick to dry, (2) they impart a fresh, pleasant scent to a dog's coat, and (3) they help to keep a dog free from fleas.

The ribbons look like long, narrow shavings, about a half inch wide. I also use them indoors as stuffing for dogs beds, and prefer them to the expensive cushions that are on the market.

To make a dog bed, use heavyweight mattress ticking for a pillow slip. Stuff this with cedar ribbons, then close the open end by stitching, so that the ribbons and ribbon particles can't slip out. Cover this with a washable, durable pillow slip in the color of your choice. Over a long period of time, a dog will wear the ribbons down into sawdust, and then the bed is emptied and restuffed with new ribbons. I restuff a bed about every six months.

I would like to own a dog, but I am concerned about the average amount of my time (daily) that he'll require. In addition to school, I have several hobbies and am very active in sports.

A cat is a better pet choice for you. A dog's social needs (companionship in particular) are the same as yours. When you retire, maybe you'll have time for a dog.

What's a fair price to pay for a good pup?

This depends upon where you live and your breed's current social status. For reasons unknown, a few breeds are always considered fashionable and command high prices.

In the late Forties, the Weimaraner was promoted as the

"miracle dog." He was supposed to do everything short of piloting a jet. The breed proved capable of doing a number of things, but excelled in none of them, and prices tumbled. Over the past few years, the Yorkshire Terrier, St. Bernard, and Old English Sheepdog have come on very strong.

Overall, prices for most of the breeds have advanced very little (and in some cases not at all) in the past thirty-five years. When you consider the devaluation of the dollar and the advance in prices of everything else (including dog foods), most pups are selling at bargain prices. Not figuring time and labor, it costs me about $100 to raise an eight-week-old Labrador pup, or twice as much as twenty years ago. Still, good Lab pups are available for $100. In 1935, a darn good Lab pup cost about $100, and $50 bought a good Beagle pup. The same dollar amount applies today.

In dollars and cents, or dollars and sense, pups (in most breeds) are the best bargains around.

How do you rate the Border Collie and why isn't this breed recognized by the American Kennel Club?

This is a good all around breed, very intelligent, and pups are usually available at reasonable prices. They are a little small for heavy work like sled pulling, however, so if you have that thought in mind, go to one of the breeds developed for that purpose: Samoyed, Siberian Husky, and Alaskan Malamute.

The A.K.C. will probably grant recognition to the Border within the next decade. Right now, the breed is one of twelve which compose a sort of A.K.C. subdivision of breeds, all rated as miscellaneous. All are candidates for recognition.

It's a sticky wicket. With 116 breeds, the A.K.C. already has its hands full, and a few of those recognized breeds (once quite popular) are now rare: English Foxhound, Harrier, and Sussex Spaniel. If those breeds were to be dropped, their owners, although few in number, would cause a mighty uproar and go to the Supreme Court for reinstatement.

The Border Collie is the oldest of the breeds developed for sheepherding. A good one carries a broad skull and a short, blunt muzzle, similar to the old-fashioned Collie's. An adult stands about

*The Border Collie is the oldest of the breeds developed
for sheepherding.*

eighteen inches and weighs forty-five pounds. Coat is black, long and wavy.

The other miscellaneous breeds: Akita, Australian Cattle Dog, Australian Kelpie, Bichon Frise, Cavalier King Charles Spaniel, Ibizan Hound, Miniature Bull Terrier, Soft-Coated Wheaton Terrier, Spinoni Italiani, Staffordshire Bull Terrier, and Tibetan Terrier. I am aware of only one book that covers them all: *The Pleasures of Dog Ownership*. If your library doesn't have it, complain and organize a sit-in. I might join you.

My dog's health is fine, but his coat is always dry and full of dandruff. Have tried several coat care preparations, but none work.

The condition is improved from the interior, not the exterior. For every twenty pounds of dog, add a tablespoonful of fat to his daily ration. Simple fats: bacon grease, lard, suet, and peanut oil. Expect improvement within twenty days. Some dogs need more fat in their diet than others. Caution: be sure to check dog's dry skin. If it shows signs of infection, run for the vet.

The simplest way to weigh a dog is to pick him up and step on scales. Assume, for example, that the total weight is 140 pounds. Next, weigh yourself without the dog. Assume your weight is 110 pounds. Subtract your weight from total weight. In this case, the dog weighs about thirty pounds, right?

Assuming that he remains in the best of health, what is the life expectancy of the average dog?

Longevity for the average dog (thirty to forty pounds) is fourteen years. Sometimes longer for lighter dogs, and almost always a few years less for the heavy breeds. In any given breed, the individual dogs who take the longest to develop into full maturity (up to three years in some cases) surpass the average life expectancy for the breed.

When an old dog fades, he does so in an almost imperceptible fashion for about a year. Then, during the next eight months, he fades rapidly: his muscle tone declines and he loses control of his bladder. Arthritis may pain him. It's time to be humane and have him put to sleep.

Longevity for cats is pegged at seventeen years; for humans, seventy years. All these figures relate to the United States.

The canine record for longevity still belongs to an English dog who died thirty-five years ago at the age of twenty-seven. He weighed about sixty-five pounds. The oldest cat on record survived in Los Angeles for thirty-three years.

How does one train a dog to stay out of a vegetable garden?

I don't know, but it must be time-consuming. My solution has always been to enclose my garden with a fence. An electric fence

68

will keep out a horse or a cow, but a dog will go over or under it.

Dogs are not intelligent enough to respect off limit signs. The world is their pasture. Either contain the dog or protect the desired property.

For individual trees and bushes, there are dog repellent sprays, but I don't know of any that are really effective. When one of these does work with a dog, application must be frequent and after every rain.

Never overestimate a dog's appreciation of value, or his consideration of your labors in his behalf. At any age, and usually out of boredom, he may chew the leg of an antique chair, enlarge the entrance to his house, or destroy one side of his sleeping bench.

There's not much you can do about the indoor items, beyond scolding and whacking the dog when you catch him in the act. Most will get the point—but they will also forget the point and have to be reminded all over again at some future date.

To discourage a puppy or an adult dog from chewing on his bench, doorway, or gate to his run, I cover the damaged surface with tabasco sauce, a paste made from dry mustard, cayenne pepper, or Kirkman's soap. A dog doesn't like the taste of any of those four items, and the same goes for a horse. Of course, the bitter taste doesn't last forever. At the first sign of new damage, I slap on a new coating of one of the anti-chews named above.

From the canine point of view, is there any real reason why dogs shouldn't live in the city?

No. The canine is an adaptable animal and quite content to live wherever man lives: any place and in any climate.

Obviously, the city isn't the ideal place for the big breeds, because, to stay in condition, all need plenty of running.

As a pup, my dog was full of fun and aggressive. Now he is two years old, shy, and afraid of people and strange noises. Since I was very careful about his training and health, how could this happen?

I would guess that you were too careful, in the way that a mother might try to protect her only child against all the dangers in the world. While your dog will never lose all of his shyness, he'll lose a great deal of it if you get him out into the world and expose him to strangers and noises. Ask people to pet him, and console him when a factory whistle blows nearby. If possible, and even if he has his basic commands down pat, enter him in obedience training classes, where he'll become accustomed to both strangers and their dogs.

Let's hope that you aren't a shy person. A dog will often pick up his master's traits. If you are a naturally nervous type, chances are that your dog won't be the calmest dog in town. If you hide in a closet during a thunderstorm, your dog might decide that storms should be feared.

My dog is obedient most of the time, but seldom when dinner is on the table. I find his begging antics amusing, and so do some of our guests, but my parents always become annoyed. Is there an easy way to teach a dog not to beg?

The begging dog seems to be one of the great social problems of our time. You have every right to spoil your dog, but not at the expense of others. If your dog is obedient most of the time, then you aren't being firm enough at dinner time.

Put him on a down-stay or sit-stay at a safe distance from the table and punish him when he breaks. If you can't bring yourself to do that, toss him into a crate or confine him in another room. The dog is a social animal, but that doesn't mean that he's our social equal.

"Safe distance" means ten feet away, or out of the reach of guests who sometimes like to slip a tidbit to a dog. Those guests don't usually own dogs of their own, and think they are being kind to the dog. So thoughtless guests are often as big a problem as a begging dog, in that they encourage the dog to beg. My dogs are trained to leave the room whenever food is served. Their reward for good conduct is the opportunity to lick plates, pots and pans after the table has been cleared.

One's guests, of course, are never responsible for the dog who jumps up on them (or their car) upon arrival. The dog means no harm, of course, and it's just his way of extending a warm welcome, but his antics are seldom appreciated.

A visitor who knows dogs will bring up one knee and bang it into the leaping greeter's chest. Thank him.

More often than not, even a well-trained dog will neglect his commands and manners in the excitement of greeting (and sometimes knocking down) a visitor. The quickest cure is to anticipate the visitor's arrival and put the dog on leash. As the dog leaps, utter a firm no and apply a firmer yank on the leash. You won't hurt the dog, but he may turn a somersault and land on his head. A few such experiences usually work wonders.

A visitor who knows something about dogs will often bring up one knee and bang it into the dog's chest. Since any sort of discouragement helps, thank the visitor.

What do you think about the obedience training schools? The lady I bought my pup from suggested one as the quickest way to train him.

Dog training schools are increasing in numbers, a pretty good indication that they are successful. Most courses run eight weeks, one lesson per week, and tuition for owner and dog is usually under twenty dollars.

While they are called dog training schools, they are really people training schools. Owners are taught particular ways in which to train their dogs, usually one command per lesson. The group method is used: a dozen owners are trained to handle their dogs at one time. For dogs, this amounts to group therapy, because they get used to the society of other dogs and other people.

The key to success depends upon the individual owner. His money goes down the drain if he depends on the one lesson per week. In addition, he must train his dog daily at home. There's instant everything these days, but not instant dog training.

My sister and I co-own a Golden Retriever. He's a beauty, and people have been encouraging us to exhibit him at a dog show. These shows have always been a mystery to us. What do we do first?

There's nothing complicated about showing a dog, but it's a long story and this is not a long book. Write the A.K.C. for a free booklet on the subject, as listed in SUPPLEMENTAL TIPS. Or check with a local person who exhibits dogs. The woods are full of dog

The moment some dogs see a camera they become ham actors.

fanciers (owners who show their dogs), and the sports editor of your local paper will know who they are in your area.

How does one prevent a bitch from going through false pregnancies?

By spaying her. False pregnancy is really a sign of good health and thus nothing to worry about. It's fairly common. If a bitch has been bred during her season, the normal gestation period (until whelping her pups) is sixty-three days, give or take a day. If she has not been bred, she often acts as if she has been anyway: her breasts swell, she usually carries milk, and she tries to dig a nest.

The maternal instinct of one of my veteran bitches is so strong that she goes into false pregnancies at least twice a year, plus whenever another pregnant bitch is about to whelp puppies. Several times, when a litter has been very large, the veteran has served as a wet nurse, taking over both the nursing and care of several of the new pups. This puts less strain, of course, on the real mother. For the medium size and big breeds, six or seven pups constitute an ideal litter. Then every pup gets enough of the dam's milk and a good start in life. When a litter runs ten, twelve or more pups, and the owner doesn't provide supplemental feedings, you can be sure that some of the pups will suffer and be weaklings all through their lives.

Is it true that dogs have a sense of humor?

Attributing human qualities to dogs has a name: anthropomorphism, a sinful word to most canine authorities and literary critics. I suspect that many of the latter have never owned dogs.

I vote yes. Just ask any owner of a Poodle, Labrador, Sealyham, Old English Sheepdog, or Dachshund. The moment one of my dogs sees a camera, and even when it's not pointed at him, he becomes a ham actor and clowns all over the place. At all other times, he's rather sedate.

My family has always owned dogs, and now my parents and I are thinking of becoming breeders (on a small scale) of Standard

74

Schnauzers, perhaps one or two litters a year. We would hope to make an annual profit, of course, but could my parents claim any loss as a tax deduction?

You're talking about a hobby kennel, and disregard what owners of hobby kennels may have told you. A hobby kennel is a fine family project, provides a community of interest, and negates the chances of a generation gap. But of the many thousands in this country, only a few make an annual profit.

To claim an annual loss as a tax deduction, you must keep very precise books and establish the intent to make a profit. The latter is done in many ways: by advertising, by exhibiting, by using business letterheads, and by building kennel facilities.

If you're lucky, the government will accept your intent and permit the loss as a business deduction. However, you can't go on declaring losses year after year. I know somebody who got away with it for five years, but that's about the limit.

The surest way to make money in the dog game is to run a boarding kennel. It takes pennies a day to feed a dog, but you charge dollars a day. In almost every part of the country, there's a shortage of good boarding kennels. If your family is looking for a private gold mine, check state laws and local zoning laws for requirements.

My grandfather has snapshots of a small, white dog he owned as a boy, and I'd like to find one. The dog was a Spitz. Is the breed still around?

Yes. The breed resembles a pint-sized Samoyed, and in the United States it is now known as the American Eskimo. It's one of several pure breeds not recognized by the A.K.C., but fully accredited by the United Kennel Club (Check in SUPPLEMENTAL TIPS.)

What do the terms "goose rump" and "foul color" mean?

Neither apply to a goose. Goose rump: the dog's rear slopes severely and his tail is set much too low. Foul color: a coat term, meaning that a purebred dog's coat color or markings do not meet the specifications of his breed standard; a white Boxer, a black

75

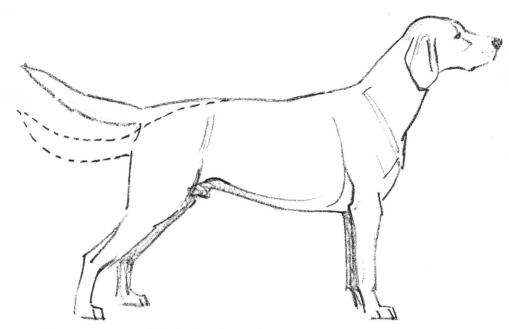

The broken line indicates a goose rump.

Samoyed, a spotless Dalmation. If you like to play word games, check INSIDE INFORMATION for some other oddball canine terms.

On any trip of over fifty miles, my dog is sure to become car sick. Is there something I can give him to overcome this?

This is motion sickness, something like the sea sickness suffered by many humans. The mode of travel is an unnatural one for the dog, so don't blame him.

Your vet can prescribe something to overcome the dog's nausea, but try a couple of other things first. Are you feeding the dog before the journey? If so, don't. If an empty stomach doesn't cure him, then try stopping every forty-five miles and taking him for a five-minute walk.

A puppy who is started on short motor trips seldom has any trouble as an adult. A healthy kitten or cat never has any trouble. The cat's inner ear is still a mystery, but somehow it protects him against both motion and altitude, and gives him his great sense of balance.

Only fools permit their dogs to get close to an open window of a moving car. Most dogs want to stick their heads out the window. They probably enjoy the breeze, but a flying particle can blind one eye for life. A silly pup, of course, will climb right through an open window. Then it's good-by for him!

Summer travel calls for a couple of extra precautions. When you must leave the dog alone, as when stopping for lunch at a roadside restaurant, be sure that (1) the car is parked in the shade, (2) doors are locked to prevent possibility of opening, and (3) windows are left open a couple of inches from the top to provide adequate air circulation. The sun's rays build up heat very quickly inside a closed car, and it doesn't take long for a dog to suffocate. Thousands of dogs perish this way every summer.

My dog is too friendly. He'll approach anyone, and several times he followed strangers to their homes. Each time, they've phoned and I've picked him up. Punishing him hasn't worked.

You are asking for your dog to be stolen. Either confine him or enlist the aid of a few strangers to whack him and then chase him home. Thus far, you've been lucky. Some strangers aren't honest and considerate.

Incidentally, your name and address should be on your dog's tag, but not his. When friendly Fido hears a stranger use his name, he's apt to put complete trust in that person. This makes things a lot easier for a dognapper.

Is it possible for a pup to have two fathers?

No. A pup can have only one father. On the other hand, other pups in the same litter can have different fathers. If mama was permitted to run free during her season, this often happens.

Which is the proper term: purebred or thoroughbred? I've seen several stud dogs advertised in the magazines as thoroughbreds.

While both terms mean the same thing, or a long line of pure-

Simply place a ruler flat across his withers and measure vertically to the ground.

blooded animals, a purebred is always a dog and a thoroughbred is always a horse. Thus, a man who is uninformed calls his dog a thoroughbred. Dogs and horses couldn't care less about the terms.

What is the difference between withers and shoulder blades?

The highest point of the shoulders, immediately behind the dog's neck, is the withers. A dog's height is measured from the withers to the ground, with the dog standing.

To measure your dog, simply place a ruler flat across his withers and measure vertically to the ground. Unless your dog is a pure-

78

bred, his adult size is unimportant. Even then, his size is really unimportant unless you intend to show him. All the breeds have recommended size ranges, and in several the range is very specific. A Brittany Spaniel, for example, is disqualified for showing if he stands under seventeen and one-half inches or over twenty and one-half inches. Thus, a very fine Brittany can miss becoming a champion by a scant quarter of an inch. That quarter inch has saddened many owners—but their dogs have remained happy.

2

Inside Information

THERE IS no absolute authority on the subject of dogs, although I know a few hundred people who have owned a couple of dogs and would disagree with that statement. One good reason for the lack of a real authority is canine research. While it is miles ahead of feline research, it still has a long way to go. Research depends largely on grants from the big foundations, and each grant is for a specified purpose. In the past decade, there has been plenty of money around for the study of cancer in dogs, but very little for the study of the canine eye. Thus, our knowledge of the canine eye hasn't increased much over the years.

Since you've read this far, it's only fair to present my own credentials. My first playmates were dogs. I've been associated with dogs all through my thinking years, and that's why I don't write about elephants. I've bred, raised, and trained hundreds of puppies. I do keep abreast of canine research, both here and abroad. But for the most part, I depend upon what I've learned from practical experience. Some of the things you'll find on these pages you won't find anywhere else, but you can bet your last dollar that they're sound. Now, about those lady dogs who haven't been spayed:

Confinement of Bitches in Season
An unspayed bitch comes into her first season any time after her first six months, and usually every six months thereafter. I've

80

owned a few who came into season annually, and just one who repeated every fourteen months.

Each season lasts about twenty-one days, but she can only be bred, and is very anxious to be bred, during a period of about six days. This period usually begins on the ninth or tenth day—but it can happen much sooner or a little later.

Except for the nonconformers, the season begins with a swelling of the bitch's vulva and the dripping of a red fluid. She is ready for breeding when the fluid becomes colorless and she flags (placing her tail to one side at the approach of another dog of either sex). The termination of the breeding period is marked by the return of the red fluid. She no longer flags and there's less of the fluid with each passing day.

If there's an adult dog in the family or the neighborhood, he will signal the approach of the heat season about ten days in advance by fooling around and flirting with the bitch. His prediction is based on strong scenting power, not ESP.

To avoid any chance of an accidental breeding, and to keep the population of strange, visiting dogs to a minimum, a bitch in season should be confined. Indoors, either a crate or a small room will do, but she should be kept on leash whenever she must go outdoors. If she is to be confined in an outdoor run, then the run should be covered with wire. She may not be big enough to jump out, but some strange dog might be able to scale the fencing and join her. Very few dogs can clear six feet, but a medium-sized dog with romance on his mind will jump four feet or so, snake one elbow over the top, and then pull himself up, over, and into the run.

Obviously, the big danger period occurs during the six days when the bitch is anxious to mate. No matter how well trained she is, she'll become an escape artist, and any dog she finds will serve her purpose.

You'd be surprised to know the number of people who just tie a bitch to the back door, tell her to be good, and leave her there unsupervised for a couple of hours. If the bitch can't chew her way to freedom, some dog is bound to come along. Her idea of being good is to mate. Almost always, unwanted puppies are the result.

Years ago, one of my bitches spent the night chewing her way through a wall of her kennel. By the time I awakened and looked out the window, the hole wasn't quite big enough for her to escape. She had been bred the previous day, but some bitches refuse to be satisfied. Canine sex instinct is very strong.

Check List for Puppy Buyers

When buying a puppy, the place to look for quality at a fair price is at a kennel owned by a breeder. A kennel cannot be defined by size alone. A big one can have several kennel buildings and a hundred dogs. A small one can be in a breeder's kitchen and contain just the brood bitch and her pups. The vast majority of kennels are small ones, running up to six or seven dogs, and producing a couple of litters of pups a year. The small kennel is usually a hobby, the puppy prices are realistic, and the owners (usually a wife and husband) hope to break even. They are interested in finding happy homes for their pups. Money in the bank is important, but secondary.

The hobby kennel is the best one to find: the one that does not provide the owners with their major source of income. These people are dog lovers, not professional sales experts. The longer they have been in dogs, the better the pups—assuming, of course, that the breeders know what they are doing. Breeders who talk a mile a minute and glow with enthusiasm, rather than price, are the ones to avoid.

Usually, you'll be able to see both parents of the puppies. This will give you a fair idea of what the pups will look like as adults. You'll get a better idea if you can see the grandparents, but that's not always possible. Still, one or two might be on the place, and the others living close by. No harm in asking.

A minority of these hobby kennels aren't firstclass, of course, but it doesn't take long to spot them: pups are dirty, pen is messy, and there's a strong smell of dog in the air. Run for the next kennel on your list. If the puppies and their surroundings are clean, take a long look at all of the pups, and a very close look at any pup who seems shy. If that pup's eyes are watery or his nose is running, chances are that he's sick, and the other pups will be sick tomorrow. If the pups are round and fat, they are getting a bum

82

start in life and are probably full of worms.

Sooner or later, and maybe the first time, you'll find a clean, healthy litter of puppies. None of these pups will grow at the same rate. If there's a runt in the litter, he may end up as the giant of those present. Almost always, you can count on a medium-sized pup in the litter to be a proper size for the breed as an adult. Then:

1. Select an aggressive pup. A shy one may be more appealing, but (even if healthy) he'll be more difficult to train.

2. Don't buy the pup unless the breeder agrees, in writing, to return your money if your vet finds anything drastically wrong with the young animal (within a specified time limit).

3. Don't bring the pup home (a) before he's eight weeks old and (b) until after he has been wormed and received his temporary shot against distemper, both at the breeder's expense.

4. Follow the breeder's instructions as to feeding. A change in diet is sure to bring on diarrhea.

5. Be sure the breeder signs and gives you the puppy's individual A.K.C. registration paper. Put it in a safe place. It's your proof of ownership.

Dogs and Cats

They have a common ancestor in Miacis, who roamed the earth some thirty million years ago. Scientists figure that he sported an ugly head, a long body, short legs, and weighed under fifty pounds.

Today, the anatomies of dogs and cats are not alike. The cat is a contortionist, his reflexes are superior, and his claws are faster than the dog's jaws. In a fair fight, the average cat will make mince meat out of the average dog. And that's why an intelligent dog usually has no more than one fight with a cat. Maybe he'll chase and bluff, but the dog won't come within range of the cat's claws.

Building an Outdoor Run

A run twenty feet long, five feet wide, and six feet high is about right for a dog of any size. That may seem pretty high for small dogs, but it will keep out small children and strange dogs.

83

Select a site that's partly shady. If the run must be in full sun, provide shade.

A lonely dog gets bored, he's almost sure to dig for freedom, so bare ground is not a good idea. Also, any dog is going to wear down the grass, and that means mud when it rains and a difficult surface to keep clean.

Here's the easy, inexpensive way to build a practical outdoor run:

1. Set poles about four or five feet apart. Locust poles are fine, but expensive. I use eight-foot lengths of four- by four-inch pine or cedar, and set them into the ground two feet. So that the wood won't rot, soak or paint the ends going into the ground with creosote or old crankcase oil (usually free at gas stations). Any part of pole coming into contact with earth should be coated. Metal poles can be used, of course, but they are the most expensive. Metal doesn't have to be coated.

2. To safeguard against digging, cover ground area with hog wire, allowing three-inch overlap.

3. Nail rough twelve-inch planks to the poles on all four sides of the run. Bottom edges of planks should sit tight on the hog wire, to secure it. When in place, the planks outline the run and serve as fenders for:

4. Pea (roofing) gravel spread to a depth of eight inches over the hog wire. This is the best ground cover for a run. Three cubic yards of gravel will be needed. Small gravel packs well, provides excellent drainage, is easy to disinfect, helps toughen a dog's pads and keep his nails short. Just rake the gravel level every few days. Cement and hardtop are expensive, rough on a dog's feet and elbows, and very difficult to disinfect.

5. Stretch and staple to the poles galvanized (to prevent rust) wire fencing around both long sides and the northern end of run. Chain fencing is great, but expensive. Fox or stock fencing is cheaper and just as serviceable. No matter what the wire may be, use nothing lighter than eleven-gauge. Any dog can bite through chicken wire.

6. Place gate at open end of run.

7. Place wooden bench, eight inches high, in run. Bench

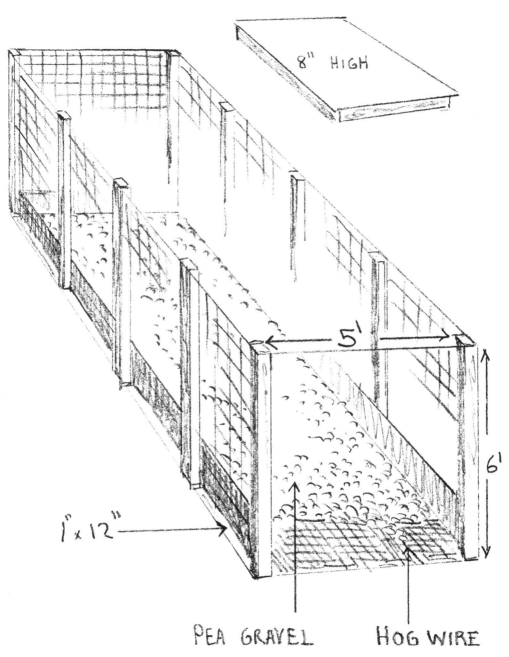

8" HIGH

5'

6'

1"x12"

PEA GRAVEL   HOG WIRE

Diagram for building an outdoor run and bench.

should be just long and wide enough to provide the dog with a place to snooze.

8. If dog is to be left outdoors most of the time, or all night, then attach doghouse to end opposite gate. A small, three-sided and roofed entrance should be provided for the doghouse, which should be placed with the open side free from prevailing winds. This will keep the house dry and the dog free from drafts.

If you have money to burn, many companies now offer kennel fencing in sections. The wire fencing is stretched on pipe frames, the frames can be bolted together, and not even corner poles are needed. The big advantage of portable fencing is that it can be moved from place to place, or from home to home. For my money, the best outfit is Mason Fence Company, Leesburg, Ohio, 54135. Sections I've bought from them have lasted for over twenty years.

You are ahead of the game if you already have an existing outbuilding with a vacant area inside on your place: garage, tool house, or shed. For protection and sunshine, use the south side of the building as the fourth side of the run, and cut an entrance.

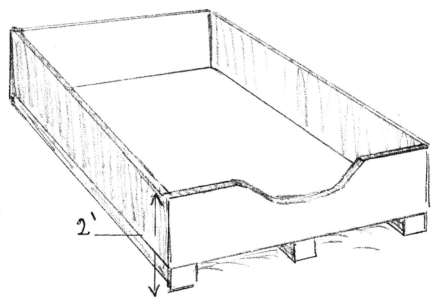

For indoor sleeping quarters, build a simple bench.

Reinforce the floor with a piece of half-inch exterior plywood, cut to fit. Slap a couple of coats of bar varnish on the finished side. This will make it easier to clean.

To prevent the pup from sticking his head out through the upright rails, and perhaps getting caught, enclose all four sides with half-inch chicken wire or hardware cloth. Then, to keep whatever litter you use from escaping, fasten ten-inch boards as bumpers along the interior sides. To keep these boards firm and upright, I attach wood strips one-half inch from both ends of two boards. These boards are placed opposite each other and provide channels for fitting in the other two boards.

Building a Low Cost Doghouse

The average lumber yard will build a doghouse for you at a cost of about thirty-five dollars for material and labor. You can cut that price in half if you are handy with a saw, drill and screwdriver.

Build the frame of two- by three-inch studs, with extra studs for floor support. Then precut and fit the floor and four sides from half-inch exterior plywood. The floor should be finished side up, and use that bar varnish again. Finished side out for the four sides. The front, of course, should have a precut entrance.

For attaching floor and sides to the frame, drill holes every six inches. Then one and a half-inch galvanized nails or, preferably, wood screws. If you try to bang a nail through plywood, you might split it.

As for the roof, a peaked one is more difficult to make and not as satisfactory as a sloped one. From front to rear, I prefer about a ten-degree slope, so framing and sides should be made with that in mind. Again, a solid piece of half-inch exterior plywood, placed finished side out, will make the roof. Measure for a one-inch overhang, sides and rear.

If you attach the front of the roof with a pair of galvanized strap hinges, and use hooks and eyes to tie down the rear, you will be able to open up the roof at any time. This will permit easier cleaning and airing.

To make this plywood doghouse waterproof, apply two coats of creosote on all four sides, and four coats on the roof. This will give you a reddish brown doghouse. If you don't like that color, wait until the creosote is dry and apply two coats of an oil base exterior house paint of a desired color.

A doghouse that sits on the ground will become too damp for its resident. The house should sit several inches above the ground, and preferably on an enclosed foundation. The cheapest and least troublesome foundation to make consists of cinder or cement blocks. Use a level to make sure that the tops of the blocks are even. The blocks do not have to be cemented together.

A dog crate can be very useful, at home as well as while traveling.

92

If the roof is sloped, and the house is set inside the dog run, it serves as a handy outdoor bench for the dog.

How to Acquire a Free, Quality Pup

The great majority of the breeders in this country own hobby kennels. Since they don't have the room or the time to care for them, they sell almost all of their pups. While the income helps to cover expenses, this is rough on their breeding program, for all know that they must have good pups coming along for the future generations.

In all breeds, some of these breeders are willing to part with fine pups of either sex on a contract arrangement known as "breeder's terms." The terms vary, but usually a happy compromise can be arranged, and no cash changes hands. In the case of a male pup, his future value depends on his status as a stud

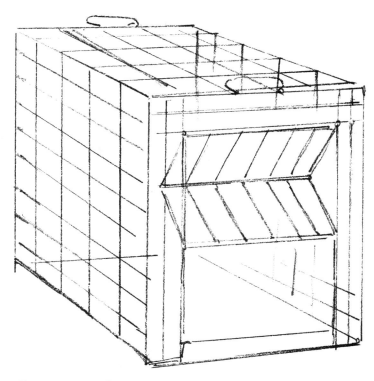

There are several types of these crates, to fit a variety of dogs.

dog. Thus, the contract might specify that the breeder will handle all the business arrangements and that stud fees will be split. In the case of a bitch puppy, the contract might specify that she be bred at a certain age, who will attend to the whelping and the raising of the pups, and how the monies derived from puppy sales will be split. In effect, you become co-owner of the pup until it reaches a certain age. At that time, you take over complete ownership.

If you look around enough, and ask about the possibility of breeder's terms, then you'll find the right pup in your favorite breed. Just be sure the contract is in writing, and that it has the full approval of your parents.

Anyone looking for a free pup and interested in the welfare of man can always tour the nearest guide dog schools for the blind. The nonprofit schools are usually looking for dog lovers who will take a pup, raise and train him according to directions, then return him to the school at about a year of age, when the dog is ready to be trained to guide the blind. When you return the dog that you took as a pup, you can, if you like, take home a new pup and begin all over again. It's a very fine thing for you to do and a great way to gain experience with many breeds. But don't become so attached to the puppy that it will break your heart to part with him.

Since not all dogs make successful guide dogs for the blind, the schools sometimes try to place the delinquents in good homes. But they are delinquents only as to guiding. Otherwise, they make good pets: healthy, trained and housebroken. At most of the nonprofit schools, these adults dogs are priced at about twenty-five dollars. If one of your parents makes out the check, this amount is tax deductible as a charity contribution.

The Money in Poodles

Wherever you live, there are plenty of Poodle owners within convenient driving distance. I wouldn't say that most Poodle owners are as lazy as I am, but the big majority of them seem to lack something—time, patience, or confidence—and they aren't interested in clipping and grooming their own dogs. They do not seem to lack money or the willingness to spend it on their dogs.

Today, my young friend Polly's profit in Poodles is paying a hefty portion of her college tuition.

Thus, keeping all the Poodle coats in shape has now become a thriving business. There are people who earn a pretty good living that way. Quite a few of them are inept, but that doesn't seem to make any difference to Poodle owners.

A few years ago, Bill Walker (eleven) and his sister Polly (thirteen) asked me if they were old enough to go into the Poodle grooming business. My answer was affirmative. I loaned them a book, told them to study it, and suggested that they look for work as apprentices (paid or not), and then experiment (for free) on neighborhood Poodles until they knew what they were doing. I thought it would take them eighteen months before they acquired enough know-how to go it on their own. Although they were unable to find work as apprentices, they followed the rest of my advice, and were confident enough to place a classified advertisement in the pet column of their local paper after only ten months.

Today, Polly is in college, and her profit from Poodles is paying a hefty portion of her tuition. Bill is still in high school, and I wish I owned his savings account. Grooming remains a spare time vocation for Bill, but now his mother and father are in the act, full time. The whole family is involved. The Walkers have branched out, in that they now handle other breeds, but most of their business comes from Poodle owners. They live on the outskirts of a small, industrial city (under 20,000 population), and they have all the business they can handle. Their Poodles rates: kennel clip —$12, show clip—$20; bath—$3, pickup and delivery—$3. Repeat business is great.

The best book on the subject is *The Complete Poodle Clipping and Grooming Book*, by Shirlee Kalstone (Howell).

Curing a Night Barker

Many dogs who live outdoors amuse themselves by barking at night, usually after the house lights are off and everybody is asleep. It may be one dog's way of complaining about his lot in life, and after awhile he'll tire and go back to sleep. Meanwhile, however, one's neighbors may become annoyed and call the police.

Run a rope from a corner post of the dog's run to the back door or a window. Near the post, attach a big, metal pail to the rope.

96

3

Supplemental Tips

MANY REFERENCES to the American Kennel Club are sprinkled throughout this book. It is a nonprofit organization, dedicated to the advancement of purebred dogs, and more the governing body of U.S.A. dogdom than it is a club. A.K.C. members are the various kennel and breed clubs scattered throughout the country, and each club is represented by a delegate. If a purebred dog is registered with the A.K.C., neither the dog nor his owner becomes a member.

The A.K.C. functions include the adoption and enforcement of rules and regulations pertaining to dog shows, field trials and obedience tests, as well as the licensing of breed judges and professional handlers, the registration of individual dogs, and setting the standard for each breed.

The address: 51 Madison Avenue, New York City, 10010.

Breed Standard
Each of the 116 breeds recognized by the A.K.C. has its own breed standard. If you are buying a purebred pup, and you intend to use the animal for some future purpose, such as breeding or showing, then it's silly not to study the standard of his breed before putting your money on the line.

The breed standard amounts to man's idea of the perfect dog in that breed. *The Complete Dog Book*, found in most libraries, is an official publication of the A.K.C. and contains the standards

101

The Norwegian Elkhound belongs to the Hound Group.

for all the breeds.

For an example of how you can go wrong: the price tag is always high for a white German Shepherd Dog pup, yet the white coat is not accepted by the German Shepherd standard.

The Best Breeds for Young Dog Lovers

Sporting Group: twenty-four breeds, all developed for the finding and retrieving of game birds. The top candidates: Golden Retriever, Labrador Retriever, English Setter, and English Springer Spaniel.

Hound Group: twenty-one breeds, developed for endurance and either scenting powers or superior vision. The candidates: Beagle, Norwegian Elkhound, and Otterhound.

Working Group: twenty-nine breeds, developed to handle various jobs, such as herding, sled pulling, or guarding. The candidates: Collie, Giant Schnauzer, Siberian Husky, and Bouvier des Flandres.

Terrier Group: twenty-one breeds, developed as bold and alert

102

dogs who would chase and burrow into the ground to find any kind of animal, or drive any game from cover. The candidates: Airedale Terrier, Border Terrier, Sealyham Terrier, Bedlington Terrier and Lakeland Terrier.

Toy Group: eighteen breeds, all developed for pleasure and companionship. In ancient times, before the invention of plumbing and any thought of a daily bath, many of these tiny breeds were used as lap dogs by members of the upper classes and royalty. Human fleas hopped from people to dogs! Unless you happen to live in a closet, and even there you might step on one, none of these breeds are for the young. They are for adults who are very careful about where they step and appreciate the fact that nice things come in small packages. But don't underestimate these featherweights: they aren't babies, and most act as if they're ready to take over the world.

Non-Sporting Group: ten breeds, developed for reasons that no

The sled-pulling Husky is one of the Working Group.

The members of the Toy Group are all developed for pleasure and companionship, like this engaging Pomeranian.

longer exist, or for no reason at all beyond companionship. The candidates: Chow Chow, Boston Terrier, Keeshound, and Standard Poodle.

Locating the Right Pup

For the names of breeders nearest you, write to Breeders' Aid care of the A.K.C. Be sure to name your breed.

Administering Medicines

Tilt the dog's head back, open his jaws with one hand, and toss the capsule or pill as far over the back of his tongue as possible. Next, hold the dog's jaws shut and stroke his chin and throat until he swallows the object.

Some dogs are great fakers, so watch him for a few minutes. He may trot off and spit out the capsule. In that case, try again.

This is the only way to give your pet a capsule. A pill can

always be mixed with his food, or hidden in a tidbit.

Medicine is spooned into a dog's mouth, and assistance is sometimes required. Lift the upper lip, about an inch off the meeting point of the jaws, and pour in the medicine. During this action, the dog's head should be held still. Afterward, hold his jaws shut and stroke his chin and neck until he swallows. If the dog doesn't like the taste of the medicine, he'll try to shake his head and get rid of it.

Preventing Ticks

There are two effective anti-tick liquids on the market. The one I use during the tick season is called Wydane, and it's available at most pharmacies. This is a concentrate, and it should be diluted as per instructions on the label. Just sponge the dog's coat. Be careful to keep the liquid away from the nose, eyes, skin and inside of ears. Also, the dog must be kept out of the sun until the coat dries, or he may suffer from sunstroke. When an animal is wet, the sun's rays have a toxic effect. You can't be careless about this fact. This tick preventative is effective for about ten days, unless the dog goes for a swim.

Tick-Tox is available only from vets. It's effective for about two days, and is more expensive in the long run. I normally use it on trips, since a dog can run in the sun immediately after application.

Breed Clubs

There's a national breed club for almost all of the 116 A.K.C. recognized breeds. Some publish magazines, others publish newsletters, and all are fine sources for finding out about available pups, stud dogs, specialty shows, and general information about a particular breed. Many of the national clubs have regional clubs that may be closer to your home. For information on the breeds named as the best breed candidates for young dog lovers, write the Secretary of:

Golden Retriever Club of America
RR #1
Constantine, Michigan 49420

English Setter Association
12625 Farndon Avenue
Chino, California 91710

Collie Club of America
72 Flagg Street
Worcester, Massachusetts 01602

Airedale Terrier Club
405 West Avondale Drive
Greensboro, North Carolina 27403

Bedlington Terrier Club
Bayberry Road, R.D. 2
Princeton, New Jersey 08450

Keeshound Club of America
9 Sunset Road
Darien, Connecticut 06820

Labrador Retriever Club
P.O. Box 1392
Southampton, New York 11968

English Springer Spaniel Club
9124 Oak Park
Morton Grove, Illinois 60053

Siberian Husky Club
3726 West Thomas Road
Phoenix, Arizona 85019

American Sealyham Terrier Club
3504 Lancer Drive
West Hyattsville, Maryland 20782

Chow Chow Club
114 Laurel Road
Chargrin Falls, Ohio 44022

Poodle Club of America
Route 1
Moore, South Carolina 39369

Border Terrier Club
Box 276
North Windham, Connecticut 06256

National Beagle Club
Wagon Wheels Kennels
Keswick, Virginia 22947

Norwegian Elkhound Association
Elkins, New Hampshire 03233

Boston Terrier Club
11951 Azure Place
Los Angeles, California 90049

Bouvier des Flandres Club
RD 2, Box 15
Front Royal, Virginia 22630

For readers dedicated to some of the other very popular breeds, write the Secretary of:

German Shepherd Dog Club
17 West Ivy Lane
Englewood, New Jersey 07631

Irish Setter Club of America
204 Cumley Terrace
Leonia, New Jersey 07605

Great Dane Club of America
73 Larchmont Avenue
Waterbury, Connecticut 06708

St. Bernard Club of America
Emmans Road, Rt. 1, Box 283E
Flanders, New Jersey 07836

Doberman Pinscher Club
12110 South 93rd Ave.
Palos Park, Illinois 60464

The Bernese Mountain Dog has characteristics of the St. Bernard and the Collie.

American Boxer Club
807 Fairview Blvd.
Rockford, Illinois 61107

Unusual Breeds

Unusual in the sense that there aren't very many of these dogs around, although all make fine pets and deserve more popularity. Many dog lovers aren't aware that these breeds exist, although they have been in this country for a long time. If you're looking for the unusual, and for a dog who will supply you with endless dinner conversations, here are the best of the unusual breeds and where to write if you're interested in more information or a pup:

Bernese Mountain Dog. Although not related to either breed, he's a smaller version of the St. Bernard and about the size and weight of a Collie. Sports a black and tan coat, with white markings. One of the original wagon pullers. The breed is recognized by the A.K.C. Write: Sanctuary Wood Kennels, Drain, Oregon 97435.

108

Clumber Spaniel. One of the heaviest spaniels (fifty pounds), very popular in this country a century ago, and a slow mover. Just right for anyone who likes to hunt—but not hurry. Recognized by the A.K.C. Write: Andronicus Kennels, Indian Ledger Road, Voorheesville, New York 12186.

Scottish Bearded Collie. The breed is not related to the popular Collie, but was developed as a sheepdog. A shaggy dog, he runs up to twenty-four inches at the shoulders, consumes about two dollars worth of food a week, and pups, when available, are priced high (three hundred dollars). I hope to own one some day. The breed is recognized by the Kennel Club (England) but not (as yet) by the A.K.C., in the United States. Write: Heathglen Kennels, 19 Gates Road, Simsbury, Connecticut 06070.

Free Literature

Almost all of the major dog food companies offer free literature about dogs and small cost items that are helpful and interesting. Several loan films for group showings. Since all advertise their products, just find the company address and write to the Publicity Director. Request copies of the company's free literature. For a start, you might try these:

Gaines Dog Research Center, 250 North Street, White Plains, New York 10602. Request copy of *At Your Service*, a listing of

The Clumber Spaniel is just right for anyone who likes to hunt— but not hurry.

free booklets. A wonderful illustrated chart of all breeds costs twenty-five cents.

Purina Pet Care Center, Checkerboard Square, St. Louis, Missouri 63199. Offers numerous booklets, the best being *Handbook of Dog Care, Puppy Primer,* and *Dog Etiquette.*

Quaker Oats Company, Merchandise Mart, Chicago, Illinois 60654. Offers booklet, *How to Feed, Care For and Train Your Dog.*

Burgerbits, Standard Brand Sales Company, 625 Madison Avenue, New York, New York 10022. Offers pedigree forms and a unique feeding indicator that pinpoints measurements for fifty breeds.

Wayne Dog Foods, Allied Mills, Inc., 110 North Wacker Drive, Chicago, Illinois 60606. Offers immunization record, pedigree forms, gestation table and booklet, *Man's Best Friend.*

American Kennel Club. For anyone interested in dog shows: Rules apply to registration and dog shows. For those interested in obedience trials: Obedience regulations. For either activity, only purebred dogs are eligible.

Pick Of the Canine Journals

Dog magazines are published in all the free countries of the world. The United States has the most, or over one hundred. Many, however, are devoted to a single breed or a specific activity, such as coon hunting. Of the balance, most are designed specifically for the dog fancier: the person who exhibits his dogs or runs them in the obedience trials.

Of the three magazines listed below, only *Dogs* will be found on the newsstands. All three offer subscriptions, but write for rates, since they change every so often.

Dogs, 222 Park Avenue South, New York, New York 10003. The best bet for dog lovers, with special articles by canine authorities and such regular departments as book, stamps, and dog psychology.

Popular Dogs, 2009 Ranstead Street, Philadelphia, Pennsylvania 19103. More for the dog fancier, but it also covers general

110

news of dogdom and features special breed columns.

Dog World, 469 E. Ohio Street, Chicago, Illinois. For dog fanciers and breeders, but it does contain a wide range of material for dog lovers, from research news to how-to articles.

Here are some magazines relating to specific breeds. They are only available through subscription.

Collie and Shetland Sheepdog, 819 Santee Street, Los Angeles, California 90014.

The Poodle Review, 26 Commerce St., New York, New York 10014.

German Shepherd Dog Review, Box 1221, Lancaster, Pennsylvania 17604.

The Boxer Review, same address as *Collie*—(above).

Weimaraner Magazine, Box 531, Madison, Wisconsin 53701.

The American Dachshund, 1016 Cypress Way, San Diego, California 92103.

Hounds and Hunting, 142 West Washington St., Bradford, Pennsylvania 16701.

Dog Books

Sometimes, especially when you don't live near a bookstore, the quickest way to get a book is through the mail. And no bookstore, of course, can possibly stock all of the dog books. I've found the firm listed below to be fair, dependable and fast. It carries dog books of all publishers, sells at list price, and pays postage. If interested, write them for list of current dog book titles.

C & B Book House, 14 South St., Danbury, Connecticut 06810.

United Kennel Club

While the average dog lover has never heard of U.K.C., it has been around since 1898, and is only fourteen years younger than the A.K.C. In total, the U.K.C. recognizes and registers only forty-two breeds. Most are also recognized by the A.K.C., but about a dozen are not. Of the latter, the best pet breeds are the American Eskimo (Spitz), Columbian Collie, and English Shep-

111

herd. For where to find pups, write the U.K.C., at 321 West Cedar Street, Kalamazoo, Michigan 49007.

The Way Things Are

As you read these words, thousands of dogs and other animals are being cruelly mistreated, and hundreds will die within the hour; not in some primitive, backward country, but in such advanced countries as the United States of America. Much of the insane cruelty and killing is legal. It is a very sad state of affairs.

Still, things are better than they were twenty years ago, and there's hope for improvement. The relief to date, and the fight for much more relief, can be credited to the many local, state and national nonprofit organizations that are popularly known as humane societies. We all owe a great deal to these anti-cruelty groups, and if you don't think so, consider this:

A century ago, not every state had anti-cruelty laws for the protection of animals, but New York did. No state had laws to protect children: the young worked in factories for pennies a day; a man could beat the daylights out of his children, and nobody had the legal right to object.

So the New York City police were helpless (1874) when a foster mother abused her daughter so frequently and dreadfully that everybody in the neighborhood, including people who beat their own children, objected. The mother was finally arrested by a humane society agent who theorized that the anti-cruelty laws applied to all animals—domestic, wild and human. The court upheld this action. It started some deep thinking about the welfare of children, and within two years New York enacted a law for the protection of children. It was the first such law in world history. A child's life has been happily safer ever since.

There's no law that says every dog lover should support at least one humane society, but there should be. One of the most effective organizations in this country, especially at the federal level, is the Humane Society of the United States, better known as HSUS. If you can spare anything—a dime, a dollar, or a couple of thousand—send it along to the HSUS at 1604 K Street, N.W., Washington, D.C. 20006. In return, you'll receive thanks and the

Like Buffy, the right dog gives loyalty, trust, and love gladly to the right owner.

society's newsletter. The letter is an eye opener. You'll find it hard to believe what's really going on in this country.

A contribution to a humane society is deductible at income tax time, so have one of your parents make out a check. All of the societies urgently need the long green stuff, and all are deserving. You can bet your last dollar that none waste pennies and all stretch them.

Aloha!

Poets have eulogized the dog as man's finest companion, but I prefer to think of him as man's best friend. A companion demands more than bed and board, and he does not necessarily give you

113

Wise men say a writer's life is a lonely one, but I've never been lonely.

his loyalty, trust and love. Nor does he make a constant effort to please you, or grant instant forgiveness for your thoughtless deeds. The right dog does all these things and more, and almost any dog can be the right dog for you, if you give him a little training, care, and affection.

I hope that you own the right dog, or that you will own the right one tomorrow. Some of your own personality will rub off on him, and he'll share your moods. And often, as if by magic, he'll anticipate your desires. Life will be a little richer, and your memory book will glow with notes about the times you've shared.

A long time ago, when I was a pup, dogs were my first play-mates and friends. Now, as I write these words, three of my best friends are daydreaming on the rug, and a fourth is snoring under my desk. Wise men say that a writer's life is a lonely one, but I've never been lonely.

My best friends join me in wishing you and your best friend the best of everything. May you . . .

"David! Come back here with my pipe!"

Index

118